A Step by Step Guide to Making Artificial Flowers

A Step by Step Guide to Making
Artificial Flowers

Paula Critchley and Pamela Westland

HAMLYN
London · New York · Sydney · Toronto

Published by
The Hamlyn Publishing Group Ltd
London · New York · Sydney · Toronto
Astronaut House, Feltham, Middlesex, England

ISBN 0 600 38073 4

Printed in England by Chapel River Press, Andover, Hants

Contents

Introduction

Introduction

Flowers have inspired artists and poets for centuries: the sheer joy of finding the first few brave bulbs when all around them is frost and snow: the exuberance of the spring flowers, as brightly coloured as the morning sun; the mass of country garden flowers that help us celebrate the height of summer, and the deep glowing colours that keep autumn a glorious memory all the winter through.

Flowers of all kinds have inspired the designs in this book, but very few have been slavishly copied. We did not aim to make flowers the neighbours will want to touch, to see if they are real. We looked at flowers, thought about flowers, closed our eyes and visualised flowers expressed in a number of ways and a variety of materials.

The first chapter is confined to patterns for big, bold and beautiful flowers to make from layers and layers of tissue paper. They will give instant results and quick confidence. Some of these paper flowers look like huge tropical wild roses, the exotic bloom of a desert cactus, or a prize garden flower — though we are not sure which one. They are all easy and cheap enough to make for party decorations or to make the customers come running to a bazaar stall.

Crêpe paper, one of the most adaptable of materials for flower making, provided two chapters in which the flowers are most nearly 'real'. White Christmas roses, roses and harebells are shown first as crêpe paper flowers, the petals realistically curled, the buds tightly coiled; then, after dipping in wax — an old saucepan and melted household candles — with the ethereal, satiny quality of flower petals.

Fabric, too, lends itself most attractively to flower making. Starched organdie, lawn and gingham has been fashioned into flowers elegant enough for the dinner table, frivolous enough for a summer hat, and fresh enough for a summer evening. Your 'bits and pieces' bag will keep your costs down to a minimum.

Nature has provided the wherewithal for a number of autumnal designs — fir cones, beech masts, preserved leaves, seed pods that might have been discarded, all find a new lease of life in flower shapes that make a striking focal point in a table arrangement. Looking at flowers made from ivy seeds and honesty petals, or mahonia leaves and a single seed pod, it is difficult to realise that they did not grow that way.

Studying books of flower paintings and botanical drawings of flower specimens has encouraged us to see flower shapes in so many of the — unlikely — materials around us. We looked enquiringly at shells on the beach, and found that many of them have pretty petal shapes and delicate flower colourings;

at beans, seeds and pasta in the kitchen and decided that they could contribute to unusual, lively and interesting flower pictures. Other pictures, using more familiar techniques, are made from pressed and dried flowers and grasses. Some designs are as nostalgic and pretty as Victorian Valentines and others suggest themselves as a new idea for kitchen decoration.

Determined not to ignore today's feeling for mass-production, we designed a whole chapter of flowers that can be cut out six or eight at a time. Once round with a pair of scissors, one fold, one twist and you have a rapidly growing pile of flowers to decorate a cone, a hanging ball or a ring. Looking backwards again, we made a flower decoration for the top of the piano — or the stereo — a ball like a pomander, substituting cob nuts for cloves, and a holly wreath with no holly, but plenty of our leaves and flowers.

Throughout the book we have given a wealth of ideas for ways of using your flowers. We recognise that empty moment that can arise when you have a box full of flowers you have made with care — and then can't think what to do with them. Our ideas range from filling a Victorian flower dome with a natural-looking arrangement of climbing roses, to making flower shapes from Cellophane paper that cast patterns like stained glass windows; from wiring huge tissue paper flowers like traffic lights on a bamboo pole for carnival time, to making a miniature nearly-magnolia tree from crêpe paper flowers.

Perhaps most important of all, we have included a chapter called The Perfect Finish and, although it is the last chapter in the book, we recommend you to read it thoroughly before beginning any of the designs. You will find descriptions and illustrations for the neatest and easiest ways to cut out templates, bind stems, wire leaves — all the preparation and finishing touches that lift your flowers from the made-in-a-moment class into the realms of floral art — or perhaps we should say flower-making art.

1 Tissue Paper Flowers

If ever the phrase 'cheap and cheerful' had meaning, it is as a description of tissue paper. It is a designer's dream, making possible all the subtle colour combinations an artist can achieve by mixing paint. For tissue paper is available in forty different colours — not at every shop, of course, but from specialist artists' materials and crafts shops and by post. Because of this colour range you don't just buy red, but the red you want: anything from deep magenta to bright, vivid scarlet; not just yellow, but pale lemon, only just off-white, to deep, burning sunset gold. And one of the most marvellous things about it is that the wide range of shades through one colour tone with each other so beautifully. It is like taking a dark colour and mixing it with a little white, then with a little more white, and so on. Each shade perfectly complements the one lighter and the one darker. Indeed, with tissue paper it is rather difficult to make a bad colour clash.

And all this for only a tiny amount a sheet. That's why we have used tissue paper in the very first chapter. It's cheap enough to cut and come again; to experiment and, if need be, discard without too much heartbreak.

The designs are big, bold and beautiful flowers. The patterns are simple, basic shapes that even someone who is 'all fingers and thumbs' couldn't possibly describe as fiddly. And even if one of your flowers doesn't go quite right the first time, all is not lost. When she was working out the patterns, the designer says she made 'quite a number of reasonably presentable things that didn't in fact look like the finished flowers, but nevertheless did work very well on the basic principles'. Which all goes to show that with a slight slip of the pencil or scissors you might turn into a designer yourself!

Tissue paper does not have the stretching properties of crêpe paper, and so is not recommended for flowers where the curl of the leaf or the twist of a petal is all-important. That's why the flowers in this chapter go to town on colour. They were inspired by flipping through a book of illustrations of exotic flowers. Flowers like the Night-blooming Cereus, which flourishes in Latin America and Hawaii and defiantly withstands the heat of the midday sun, have distant relations on these pages.

Because of the bold colours and the large scale of the flowers, there's an air of carnival about them. Think of them in terms of instant decorations for a party or a dance. A small band of helpers could transform a room in next to no time, and these bright flowers would be as popular as balloons to take home afterwards.

Our flowers are mounted on bamboo canes, but they could

equally well be wired to strong twigs or branches – perhaps standing in the corner of a room or at the end of a hallway, in a large acid jar or plain white jug. Alternatively, you could fasten them to natural materials, such as strong stems of oats or corn, or the thick, woody stems of pampas grass.

Although, the instructions tell you to cut out the pattern shapes with scissors or serrated scissors, you might like to experiment in some cases with tearing the edges. This gives a surprisingly natural effect. Just dip a paintbrush in clean water and run it along the line you want to tear. Then, while it is still damp, tear it with little jerking movements for a pretty, vignetted look.

First in this chapter is a design for a giant wild rose – even with a designer's flair and imagination, you see, a simple four-petalled shape came first to mind. Though, in fact, the pattern is cut eight petals at a time and doubled so that there is the very minimum of intricacy about it.

Next, a set of three chrysanthemums – or are they cactus dahlias? – shown like traffic lights one above the other on a bamboo cane. Streamers dangling, they make a fun decoration stapled to a plain painted or pinewood wall. And there's a simpler version for children to make, from paper which is cheaper still.

Lastly, a huge tropical daisy, our own version of the night-blooming flower, that would be the focal point of any room. Stand a bunch of them where you would like another accent piece of furniture; in a fireplace where there's no fire; in a window to mask the view.

GIANT WILD ROSE
As you can see from the colour photograph of this flower, facing page 18, the edges look 'for real' – if there were such a thing, that is, as a wild rose 8 inches across. Children will love working out this effect. It is like magic painting. All you do is to take four layers of tissue paper, in two colours layered alternately, and paint round the edges with plenty of clear, cold water. Just like magic, the dye from both colours starts to run, and each colour picks up the one above and below it. In our flowers, therefore, the pink edges are dyed by the dark green and the green edges have a pink-tinted border.

For each flower you will need:
2 sheets of tissue paper in contrasting colours, 1 dark and 1 light (we used dark green and pale pink); pencil; ruler; pair of compasses (or something like a meat plate, with a 12-inch diameter); scissors; paintbrush; paper clips; 6 inches of fine wire; transparent self-adhesive tape; rubber adhesive; bamboo cane or other stems or twigs to mount the flower.

Before deciding which flower to photograph in colour, we tried a number of colour combinations and they all looked good. According to the colour scheme of your room, you might like to try purple and pale blue or orange; dark blue and yellow; scarlet and pale blue, deep pink and turquoise – as we have said, you can hardly go wrong.

Begin by folding the two sheets of tissue paper in half. Starting at the bottom with one half of the darker tissue, insert

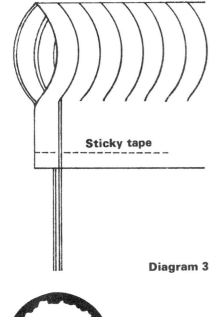

Sticky tape

Diagram 3

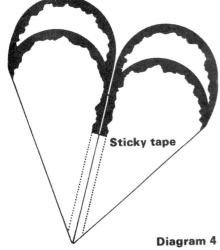

Sticky tape

Diagram 4

A

one half of the lighter tissue, then fold over the remaining half of the darker, then the remaining lighter. So that, if you are using green and pink as we did, you will have green on the bottom, then pink, green, and pink on top.

With a pair of compasses or using a meat plate as a guide, draw a circle with a 12-inch diameter. Cut through all four sheets, paper-clipping them together to hold them in position so that they do not separate.

Fold in half (all four circles still together) to give a semi-circle; in half again, so that you have a quarter segment, and again to give you an eighth section. Trace the petal shapes from Diagram 1 and cut through all the thicknesses.

Open out the circles again and lay them flat, on top of each other, on a piece of newspaper or blotting paper. You will have an eight-petalled shape.

Dip the paintbrush in cold water and 'paint' the top layer all round the petal shapes, about $\frac{1}{8}$ or $\frac{1}{4}$-inch from the edges (photograph A). Use enough water to penetrate all the thicknesses, so that each layer is dyed by the colour above or below it, as already described. Don't worry if the watery outline is uneven and slightly blurred; it is actually more attractive this way.

Place each layer out singly on newspaper to dry, for about 5 minutes, while you make the centre piece. Cut a strip 6 by 4 inches from each of two sheets of tissue, one of the lighter and one of the darker colour. Lay them on top of each other and fold in half lengthwise, so that you have a strip 6 by 2 inches. Put a dab of glue or a thin strip of sticky tape along the cut edges to keep them together.

Make $\frac{1}{4}$-inch-wide cuts over the folded edges, down to

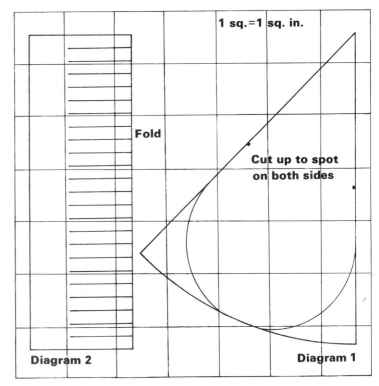

1 sq.=1 sq. in.

Fold

Cut up to spot on both sides

Diagram 2

Diagram 1

within $\frac{3}{4}$-inch of the base, as shown by the lines on Diagram 2. Insert a doubled fine wire between the first and second loops (to keep it from falling off) and wrap round the wires (Diagram 3). The flower centre should then look like photograph B. Wrap a thin strip of sticky tape round the base to secure it. This will not show in the finished flower. Continue to make the main part of the flower now that the 'painted' edges are dry.

Take each layer of tissue separately. Fold it in half so that you have a double-thickness, four-petal shape. Wrap the semi-circle round to form a cone and sticky-tape along the edges where they meet. Do not overlap them. See Diagram 4. Repeat with the other three tissue shapes, making them all into cones.

Insert one cone inside another, in the order in which the paper was cut out. Put a dab of glue on the base of a pink cone, position it inside a green cone, so that the petals of the second cone fill in the space between the petals of the first one. Repeat, finishing with a green cone. Diagram 5 shows the sequence of the petals, with the two green layers one above the other, and the two pink layers filling in the spaces in between. Push the wired flower centre into the top, pink cone.

The success of this flower largely depends on the care you take with the next stage. It will either look like four coloured tissue paper cones or a giant wild rose, according to how gently and evenly you pull out each petal.

Start with the petals in the outside, green layer, and turn them over one by one, as in photograph C. Remember that in hot countries the flowers like to turn their faces fully to the sun! Continue until all the petals are evenly opened out.

The leaf does not have a separate pattern, it is another eight-petalled shape cut from dark green tissue paper. Cut out the pattern as before (Diagram 1), fold it into quarters (giving a two-petal shape) and cut down the sides of each petal to within 1 inch of the base. If you want to make your flower look more exotic, simply cut out more petal patterns and position them one above the other down the cane.

To fix the flower on a bamboo cane, make a little vertical notch at the top of the cane, say about $\frac{1}{4}$-inch down, and push the wire well down into the cut. Bend the flower head over slightly if you want to. To position flowers further down the cane (as we have done with the chrysanthemums which follow), cut a shallow, horizontal ring with a pen-knife so that the wire has something to grip into.

To fix the leaves on the cane, wrap them round and tape them in place (Diagram 6, page 12). To hide the tape, which would show, cut a strip of the same colour tissue, about 4 inches by $\frac{1}{2}$-inch, dab a spot of glue at one end, wrap it round the stick and tape, and finish off with another dab of glue. Photograph D overleaf, shows the completed flower.

TRIPLE CHRYSANTHEMUM FLOWERS

Three of these flowers on a bamboo cane look remarkably like someone's fanciful imaginings of traffic lights — at the very least, they are bright enough to make anyone stop and look twice. As you can see from the colour photograph facing page 18, this is the designer's private joke: the centres of the

Diagram 5

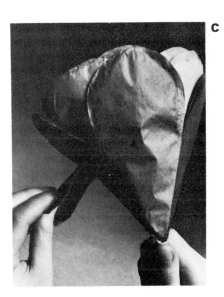

C

Diagram 6

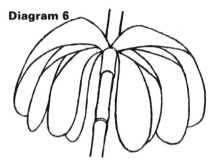

D

Diagram 7

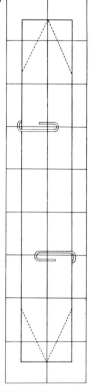

1 sq.=1 sq. in.

flowers are red, amber and green respectively!

These flowers are designed to be highly colourful, so they are not ones on which to exercise the latest fashions in muted or pastel shades. This is the time to display a childlike love of bright, even clashing tones, on the 'anything goes' principle.

You can make the flower virtually any size you like, given only the limitations of the size of a sheet of tissue paper, which is normally 20 inches wide. What is important is to keep to the proportion given in the instructions below. This is that the length is $2\frac{1}{2}$ times the width. Therefore, if the width is 4 inches, the length will be 10 inches; if the width is 6 inches, the length will be 15 inches, and so on. This pattern actually measures 8 × 20 inches.

For each flower you will need:
Tissue paper in 3 colours for the outside petals and a contrasting colour for the centre; fine wire; pencil; paper clips; scissors; bamboo cane.

Lay the four sheets of tissue paper on top of each other, fully opened out, and paper-clip all four sides to hold them together. The pattern is 20 inches wide, the width of the sheets of paper, and 8 inches long. Rule 8 inches in from each end, draw a line across, and cut through all four sheets.

Fold the paper in half, lengthwise (10 inches), in half again (5 inches), again to make a $2\frac{1}{2}$-inch strip and for the last time, $1\frac{1}{4}$ inches.

Paper-clip the strips together again to hold the four layers in position and draw in the dotted lines from the pattern to show you where to cut the points of the petals (see Diagram 7). Cut along the four dotted lines, through all thicknesses, with very sharp scissors.

Carefully unfold the entire length of the four pieces of paper and re-fold concertina fashion, using the creases as guides.

With the central colour uppermost, fix a 10-inch wire round the centre of the fan, without squashing the paper. Twist it three or four times to secure, and let the remainder hang away from the central colour. Then spread out like a fan.

Gently ease up the first layer of tissue (the one nearest the middle) until it stands up in points, taking great care not to tear it (see photograph E). Repeat on the opposite side. Gradually ease up all four layers on both sides. Try to get it as bunched up in the middle as you can, to make a nice fluffy centre.

Make as many flowers as you require. Wire them on to a bamboo stick in the manner described for the Giant Wild Rose.

For a real carnival effect, cut streamers from single layers of tissue paper, cut an inverted V shape in the ends and stick to the cane (photograph F).

TISSUE CARNATION FOR CHILDREN TO MAKE
No-one should be too proud to accept help and advice. . . . When the designer was working on the patterns for this book, her windowcleaner knocked on the window and rather bashfully told her that he could make paper flowers. His grandmother had taught him. So here is the result: a simpler, but equally attractive version of the chrysanthemum flower.

made from multi-coloured toilet roll tissue.

Obviously these flowers cannot have the flamboyance of colour or the size of the others, but they are fun for children to make on a dull, rainy afternoon. We have seen them used to decorate the top and sides of a bazaar stall, alternately in pink and blue, where we have to report they not only drew customers to the stall but gave rise to enquiries on their own behalf.

E

For each carnation you will need:

2 lengths of double strength toilet roll tissue with 2 sections in each (do not tear down the serrated edge); hair grip or fine wire.

Place the two sections of tissue one on top of the other, as shown in Diagram 8, page 14. Starting at one end of the narrow side, fold into a concertina shape all down the length, making each fold about 1 inch wide.

Slip a hair grip over the centre to hold it in place, or twist a piece of fine wire round, being careful to keep the width of the paper and not squash it (Diagram 9).

F

To spread out into a fan shape and pull up the layers, follow the directions for the chrysanthemum flower, taking care not to tear the paper. If the paper is rather difficult to get hold of, it makes it easier if you blow on the layers to separate them (photograph G). The result, in a matter of minutes: a carnation! (photograph H.)

To give a little more personality to the flowers, you can experiment with dyeing the tips of the petals.

If you have any coloured Indian ink, put about a teaspoonful into an old saucer with about three times the quantity of water. Mix it well and very gently dip the edges of the petals into the liquid. Leave the flower to dry upside-down. You can try the same technique using poster paints or water-colour paints, mixed up to a very watery consistency. Test the colour first of all on a sheet of paper to see whether you are going to like the effect.

G

TROPICAL DAISY

This is the flower that owes its inspiration to an exotic South-American plant, so buy the brightest tissue you can find and prepare to make an impact.

For each flower you will need:

1 sheet of dark tissue (such as black, dark blue, purple or dark green) from which to cut 2 circles with a 4-inch diameter; 1 sheet of tissue paper for centre (ours was bright pink); 2 sheets tissue paper for petals (ours was scarlet); tracing or greaseproof paper; about 7-inch length fine wire (rose wire); rubber adhesive; pencil; ruler; pair of compasses; transparent self-adhesive tape; paper clips; ordinary scissors and ones with serrated edges (pinking shears) if available; sticking plaster.

This flower has 2 centres, one small, dark one (ours was black) and one larger (pink) one.

To make the pink centre, fold the whole sheet of tissue paper, which is 30 by 20 inches, into four until it measures 10 by 15 inches. With a pair of compasses (or a plate the appropriate size) draw a circle with a $7\frac{1}{4}$-inch diameter on the

H

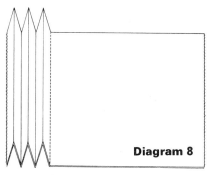

Diagram 8

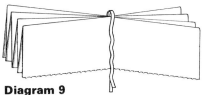

Diagram 9

Diagram 11

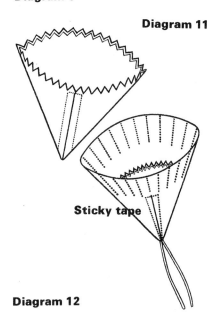

Sticky tape

Diagram 12

top layer. Cut through all four thicknesses. Paper-clip the four pieces of paper round the edges with two or three clips. Keep the circles in position and fold them in half to make a semi-circle and then once again, making a quarter. Using tracing paper or greaseproof paper (which is cheaper and more readily to hand in most households), trace Diagram 10(a). Sticky-tape the tracing, pencilled side down, in place over the quarter circle and draw over the lines to mark in the necessary cuts. Cut down each line, preferably with serrated scissors.

Now unfold the paper until you have a semi-circle again. Cut a small strip of sticky tape, about $2\frac{1}{2}$ inches long. Form the semi-circle into a cone shape so that the folded-up sides meet but do not overlap. Secure them with the strip of tape, as shown in photograph I.

Next, fold the small piece of dark (black) tissue paper in half and draw a circle with a 4-inch diameter. Cut out two circles, preferably with scissors with a serrated edge. Form into a cone as before (Diagram 11), securing with a strip of sticky tape. Dab some rubber adhesive at the base of the small black cone, about $\frac{1}{2}$-inch all the way round, then stick it firmly into the pink cone.

Now take a piece of fine wire about 6 or 7 inches long, double it and make a loop round something like a pencil, twisting it underneath a few times. Insert the doubled wire through the centre of both cones (Diagram 12). The loop will hold it in position.

Next you make the outside petal shape. Place two sheets of tissue paper one on top of the other and fold in half to make 15 × 20 inches. Draw a circle with a 13-inch diameter. (This is about as wide as the average pair of compasses will stretch.) Paper-clip the four thicknesses together to keep them steady and cut through all four layers. Fold in half and then into quarters, as you did for the larger centre piece.

Trace Diagram 10(b) for the petals, again sticky-taping over the quarter-circle of tissue paper. Cut these with ordinary scissors. After cutting, unfold the layers completely until they are flat circles again and, keeping your compasses point in the centre of all four, very slightly move each layer round so that the petals no longer fall exactly on top of each other. Then re-fold into one semi-circle.

Diagram 10c

	Fringed leaf								
	1 sq.=1 sq. in.								

You want to make this piece into a cone as before, but this time sticky-tape the edges on the inside so that the taping will not show. Use a strip of about $3\frac{1}{4}$ inches of sticky tape.

Now fit the smaller cones into the big one (photograph J) and stick the wire right through. Twist the wire around two or three times underneath.

To mount the flower on a bamboo cane, follow the directions given under Giant Wild Rose. It might be easier, for balancing purposes, to wire just the very end of the cone shape flat to the bamboo. Take about the last $\frac{1}{2}$-inch of it, because the leafy fringe will just cover this.

To make the leafy fringe, cut a piece of tissue paper 7 by 12 inches. Choose any colour you like, but preferably one which contrasts with the colours you have used for the flower.

Fold the paper in half lengthways, then twice more, to make a strip measuring 7 by $1\frac{1}{2}$ inches. Then, following the pattern in Diagram 10(c), cut down in strips, as shown, to within $2\frac{1}{2}$ inches of the base.

Bamboo canes have a slippery surface, so here is a trick to make your fringe stay put firmly. Put a little piece of sticking plaster just under the base of the flower and spread it with rubber adhesive. Now take the fringe, with the cut edge pointing towards the flower, and wrap the base, first of all, round the sticking plaster and then round the bamboo, keeping the bottom edges absolutely level (Diagram 13). Hold the bamboo at an angle, with the flower slanting down towards the floor, while you do this. Cut a small piece of sticky tape, just about 1 inch, and stick it down neatly. The glue will hold it in place. Then, when the bamboo is upright, the fringe will fall downwards over the $2\frac{1}{2}$-inch piece of tissue paper. You can repeat that at intervals of 6 inches all the way down the cane, if you like, for a lush, verdant plant (photograph K shows a finished flower).

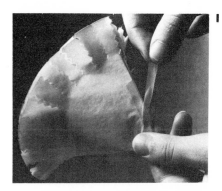

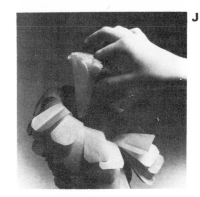

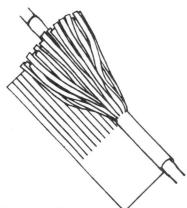

Diagram 13

1 sq.=1 sq. in.

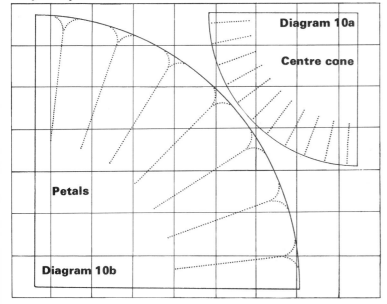

Diagram 10a

Centre cone

Petals

Diagram 10b

2 Crêpe Paper Flowers

Crêpe paper has one quality not readily found in other materials — it stretches easily and, once stretched, holds its shape. It is not subject to change in different atmospheric conditions and so any creases, bulges and curls stay put. These properties have a great advantage in artificial flower design, and make crêpe paper one of the most suitable materials when realistic, natural effects are wanted. This, then, is not the material to choose for bold, geometric shapes: although crêpe paper copes perfectly well with that type of flower, the designs do not make the most of its potential as a craft material.

Crêpe paper is inexpensive and it is essential to buy the best quality you can find. Indeed, the paper we used, sold in sheets measuring 8 feet 6 inches by 20 inches, has 'Very Best' printed on the label, just so that you make no mistake! It is available in twenty-eight colours, including such botanically-orientated names as golden rod, melon orange, buttercup yellow and mint green. But, for this chapter, we chose to use only white for the flower petals, and let the differences in shapes ring the changes and emphasise the versatility. We used the 100 per cent stretch quality for petals, and the 60 per cent stretch, which is stronger, for leaves.

The paper has two sides, one shiny and one matt, and really you can choose which you will call the 'right' side; we always chose the matt one.

Although crêpe paper has this fantastic ability to be frilled, bent, stretched, curled and pleated, it does have limitations and, in case you decide to experiment with designs of your own (or adapt others from this book) it is as well to know what they are.

You must always cut petals and leaves with the pattern on the straight grain, as you are usually advised to do when cutting material in dressmaking. That is, with the up-and-down way of the pattern running up and down the grain. Then you will curl or stretch the petals and leaves across the grain of the paper. This way, they will be responsive and the shape will be permanent. It is important to get this right at all times, and not be tempted to twist a template sideways to get another pattern cut out of the paper. The results will be disappointing and the paper will tear all too readily.

We found that circular flower patterns are not suitable for this paper at all. If you cut a circular piece and plunge a centre through it, the top and bottom will be strong, but the centre will not. The edges then need complicated wiring to hold them in shape, and the whole purpose — of designing flowers to suit the properties of the material — is lost.

If you want to work with coloured papers, you will probably

be able to find a specialist shop which stocks a large range. If not, postal services are offered by some shops. You can introduce your own variations by colouring the paper with oil paints, but not with inks. The high absorbency of the paper is a problem and with inks it just looks as if it has been left out in the rain.

To demonstrate the versatility of crêpe, we have chosen to show Christmas roses, tiny rose buds, roses, and another flower, slightly a figment of the designer's imagination, a spiky star-shaped flower, part anemone and part lily. In all of these, the curl and curve of the petals is important to the design and they are the nearest any flowers in the book come to looking 'real'.

STAR-SHAPED FLOWER

Carrying realism a stage further, we decided to show these white crêpe paper flowers wired on to natural twigs, against a cloudy-sky background. Colourful birds (you can almost hear them singing!) complete the exotic arrangement you can see facing page 22. If you decide to copy this display, you can mount it on a piece of hardboard or plywood, or an old tray, and build up a mound of moss and grasses. Alternatively, and easier to handle, you can wire the flowers on to some longer twigs and stand them in a vase. From a distance, they might look like the flowers of the magnolia which precede the leaves.

For each flower you will need:
A ball of magenta-coloured Raffene (we used colour number 21); two 7-inch fine rose wires; white crêpe paper for petals; dark green crêpe paper for fringed centre, sepals and leaves; rubber adhesive; orange stick to curl petals: scissors; card for template; pencil; tracing or greaseproof paper; ruler.

Trace the pattern shapes from the outlines in Diagram 1, reverse the tracing and transfer the shapes on to thin card such as an old postcard. Cut out the templates, one for each shape.

Wind 16 loops of magenta-coloured Raffene $2\frac{1}{4}$ inches long. Secure with one rose wire in the centre and twist three or four times underneath. Take a second rose wire and tie $\frac{1}{2}$-inch from the base, with two or three ties, so that loops are now vertical, leaving remaining wire for fringe (see photograph A). The two separate ends of the rose wire will, in fact, form the one stalk.

Trim the raffia centre into a rounded brush shape, leaving just one or two of the loops uncut. You will find that these

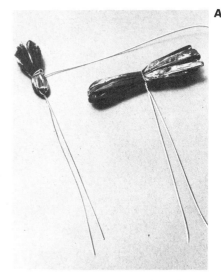

A

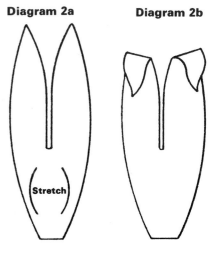

B

Diagram 2a **Diagram 2b**

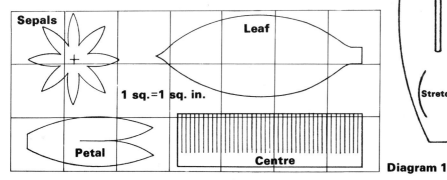

Sepals

Leaf

1 sq.=1 sq. in.

Petal

Centre

Stretch

Diagram 1

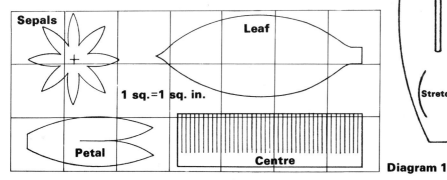

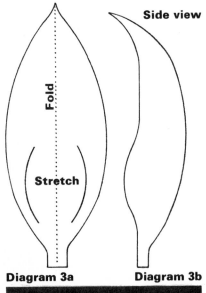

Side view

Fold

Stretch

Diagram 3a　　　　**Diagram 3b**

C

D

'catch the light' in an interesting way, giving your flower flattering highlights!

Cut out the fringed centre shape from green crêpe paper, making sure to cut it on the up-and-down grain of the paper. Cut the fringed ends, as indicated by the lines on the pattern, as close together as you can. Wrap the fringe round the wired flower centre, with the cut side upwards, and fasten with remaining wire just underneath previously wired raffia. Curl the inside fringe over the raffia and the outside fringe away, flicking the fringe out to give it a 'free' effect (see photograph B). To do this, use a very thin instrument like an orange stick or hair curling pin and wrap the inner layer over it towards the inside and the outer layer the other way.

From the white crêpe paper, cut out four of the petal shapes. Each one has two 'points' so you will, in fact, have an eight-petalled shape. Dividing one petal into two, as it were, gives less bulk at the calyx and therefore a neater finish. To cut out the petals draw round the template with a pencil on the wrong (shiny) side of the crêpe, being careful to keep the pattern straight on the grain. Cut out each petal just inside the pencilled line so that the petals do not have a dark outline.

Cut down the central line of each double petal. Stretch the petal between the base and the cut, holding it with the thumb and forefinger of both hands, and pulling it very gently into a stretched curve. (see Diagram 2(a)). Curl over the petals towards you (see Diagram 2(b)).

Using a matchstick, put a dab of glue on the base of all four petals. Stick two petals opposite each other, turning inwards, just above the wire securing the fringe. The bulge in the petals takes the shape of the raffia flower centre. Wire the petals in position. Stick the other two petals opposite each other and wire them (see photograph C). Now curl the tips of the petals towards you, that is outwards.

From green crêpe paper, cut out the star shape for the sepals. Make a cross-cut in the centre, not too big, about $\frac{1}{4}$-inch each way. Dab a little glue just above the wire and ease the sepals over the wire 'stalks', pull over 'calyx' and just cover the wire.

As you can see from the photograph, we have used leaves for only those flowers arranged in the foreground. If you want to use your flowers in a table decoration, put leaves on some but not on all — otherwise the leaves will 'swamp' the flowers.

Cut a strip of green crêpe paper, through all the thicknesses (see Chapter 9), $\frac{1}{4}$-inch wide. Use this to bind the stem of the flower down both strands of rose wire, to the bottom. To do this, use the strip single thickness and put a tiny dab of glue one end. Starting at the top, press the glue to the flower calyx and wind the strip round horizontally two or three times. Holding the stem in your left hand and twisting it gently around, wrap the paper strip horizontally down, so that each layer neatly overlaps the previous one. Put a dab of glue to secure it at the end of the stem.

Cut out a leaf pattern, also from the green crêpe paper. Secure the leaf or leaves in the following way: first fold the leaf in half and stretch it above the base. (Diagram 3(a)). Curl it back a little at the point (see Diagram 3(b)) spread a

Bright and beautiful tissue paper flowers

little glue around stalk about $\frac{5}{8}$–1 inch from the bottom, wrap base of leaf round and hold in position.

Using another strip of green crêpe paper, put a tiny dab of glue at one end and stick it on to the base of the leaf. Bind all the way down to the bottom of the stem again. Secure with a tiny dab of glue at the end. This all-in-one appearance of calyx, leaf and stem gives a neat finish to the flower.

Position the flower attractively by bending it into the bulge of the leaf and then curling it out at the top (see photograph D).

Where leaves are not to be included, simply bind the calyx and stem from top to bottom with green crêpe paper strip.

CHRISTMAS ROSE

Christmas roses – or *heliborus niger* as the gardeners know them – are extra-precious, flowering as they do in the depth of winter when very few other blossoms brave the elements. Consequently, one rarely sees them picked in quantity. Make your own, however, and you can fill a vase with as many as you like – and you don't have to go out into the snow to gather them!

You can see how pretty the flowers look in an old china creamer jug. If your china shelves do not reveal a decorated cow like this one, look instead for an old teapot, perhaps one that lost its lid years ago, a sauceboat or even a tea cup to make your arrangement. Or try laying some of the flowers, faces upwards, in a small shallow glass fruit bowl. This way they look as if they are floating on water, evoking a delicate, waxed impression.

For each flower you will need:

Sisal string; plastic-covered garden wire (or similar) for the stalk; fine wire or 7-inch rose wire; white crêpe paper; pot of gamboge yellow Indian ink; pencil; thin card for template; tracing paper or greaseproof paper; scissors; comb; rubber adhesive; white floral tape (optional).

Cut a piece of sisal $2\frac{1}{2}$ inches long and hook it in the centre with a length of plastic-covered garden wire (see photograph E). This wire will be used for the stalk, so cut it accordingly – our flowers stood a minimum of 6 inches high.

With a piece of fine wire 7 inches long or one 7-inch rose wire, secure the two lengths together $\frac{1}{4}$-inch from the base, twisting the wire three or four times underneath so that the string is now vertical.

Unravel the string with a small piece of comb, or with your fingers, and fluff it out as much as possible, separating each individual strand (see photograph E). Flatten it out until it is a smooth, round brush shape, and then cut it like this. Trim round the edges until it is a neat circle, closely crop the middle until there is a little round 'bush', leaving just a wispy, whiskery outside. Diagram 4 shows you how to do this.

Now colour the centre of your string the lovely bright yellow of real Christmas rose flowers. Put some yellow Indian ink into an egg cup or small jar and dip in the sisal centre for a few seconds. Make sure that it is completely covered by the ink. Remove and leave to dry on a piece of absorbent paper or kitchen paper for about ten or fifteen minutes. When it is

E

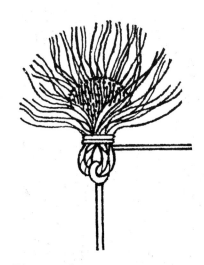

Diagram 4

dry, reshape the outside fringes inwards, so that it is very slightly cup-shaped. This will enable the petals to fit over better.

The pattern pieces are for a fully-opened flower, a bud and two sepals. Each flower and bud has five petals.

Trace the pattern outlines, Diagram 5, on to tracing or greaseproof paper, reverse the paper and go over the outlines with a soft pencil to transfer them on to thin card, such as an old postcard or used cereal packet. Cut out the shapes.

Place the template straight on the grain of the paper and cut out five petals.

Begin by making a fully-opened flower. Stretch each petal very gently as shown in Diagram 6(a). To do this, hold it just above the base with the fingers and thumbs of both hands, first one side and then the other, very carefully stretching the paper to make a bulge. You will find that you do not need to curl the petals. If you stretch them slowly enough, an 'inclination' will apear at the top, which is all you really need.

Put a dab of glue on the base of the sisal and of the petals and leave to become 'tacky' for five to ten minutes. In this time you can be cutting out the petals for another flower or a Christmas rose bud, and stretching them.

To make a bud, cut out five of the smaller petals and stretch them as described for the other petals, but slightly more in the middle of the petal shape (Diagram 6(b)). This will give a greater bulge to the flower.

Position the flower petals as evenly round the sisal centre as you can. The easiest way to do this accurately is by the 'clockwise' method. It is this: Hold the flower stem in your left hand and put the first petal with the inside facing you, in the 12 o'clock position; at the top of the circular centre, in other words. Dividing your imaginary clock face into fifths (which admittedly is not easy!) fit the next petal in the position of 12 minutes past the hour; the third at 24 minutes; the fourth at 36 and the last one at 48. Wire round the base of the petals, using the remaining fine wire and finish it off at the top of the stalk.

This flower — both the bud and the fully-opened bloom — has to be taped twice. You could use white floral tape first, or two layers of $\frac{1}{4}$-inch-wide crêpe paper strip. Tape with the first layer, from the base of the flower all the way down the stem, in the method described for the star-shaped flower.

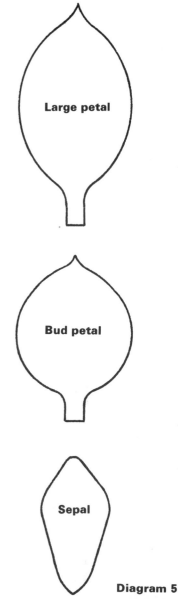

Large petal

Bud petal

Sepal

Diagram 5

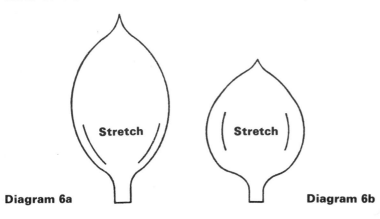

Stretch

Stretch

Diagram 6a

Diagram 6b

F

21

G

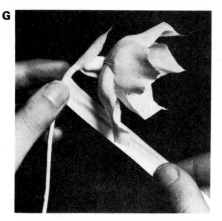

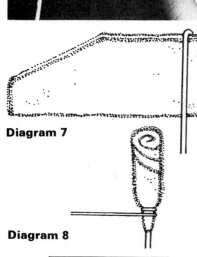

Diagram 7

Diagram 8

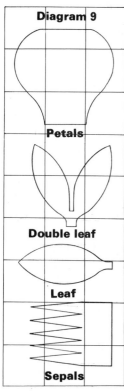

Diagram 9

Petals

Double leaf

Leaf

Sepals

1 sq.=1 sq. in.

If you are using floral tape, though, you will not need to dab the ends with glue. (See photograph F).

Next cut out two sepals and stick one on top and one underneath, at the top of the stalk just under the calyx, so that the sepals face upwards towards the flower. The underneath one will have to be slightly curled back, to allow room for the flower.

With the narrow strip of white crêpe paper, tape all the way down again, from about $\frac{1}{4}$-inch under the first tape (photograph G), securing the paper strip with a tiny dab of glue at each end.

These flowers take very well to waxing, and look even more life-like. Full instructions are given in the following chapter.

WHITE ROSES

Still with an eye firmly on the gardening books, we now have a pattern for a white rose; not a Christmas rose, this time, but the white rose of summer. It can, of course, be made in any other colour of crêpe paper you choose. We give instructions first for the rose bud, and then for the fully-opened flower.

For each rose bud you will need:

One 7-inch long florist's wire; three 7-inch rose wires and another one for each leaf; cotton wool; white crêpe paper (100 per cent stretch); olive green crêpe paper (60 per cent stretch, for the leaves); an orange stick or hair curling pin; green floral tape; pencil; thin card; tracing or greaseproof paper; scissors; rubber adhesive.

Divide a wad of cotton wool through its thickness and cut a length 1 inch high by $2\frac{1}{2}$ inches. Cut off one corner at an angle as shown in Diagram 7. Hook the end of a florist's wire at the top of the cotton wool and bend over on the other side. Wrap the cotton wool round, not too tightly, keeping the end level. Secure with two twists of a double rose wire, $\frac{1}{4}$-inch from base (Diagram 8).

Following the instructions already given, make templates for the pattern shapes (Diagram 9) and cut out the pieces from the crêpe paper. You will need four petals cut from the white crêpe paper and one sepal shape cut from the green.

To give each petal a natural-looking curl at the sides, take an orange stick or thin hair-curling pin and twist round first one side and then the other of the crêpe petal pattern. Turn the petal so that the curled-in edges are away from you, and stretch it in the centre, as already described. Diagrams 10 and 11, page 24, show you how to curl and stretch this petal.

Tightly wrap first petal, curled side out, round the cotton wool centre, which should be $\frac{3}{4}$-inch below. Secure with two twists of the rose wire (Diagram 12). Use the clockwise method of placing the petals again, to ensure accuracy. If the first petal was placed at 12 o'clock, put the next one at 15 minutes, the third at 30 and the last one at 45. Make sure to place all petals so that they are level at the top edges. Wire tightly down the base of the petals on to the stem. Now curl some of the top edges outwards, in the way described for the sides, so that they bend over very slightly (Diagram 13).

Spread a little glue on top of the wire holding the petals.

22

White crêpe paper flowers wired to natural twigs

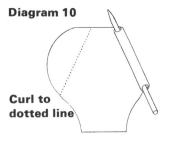

Diagram 10

Curl to dotted line

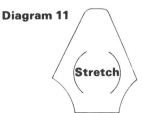

Diagram 11

Stretch

Diagram 12

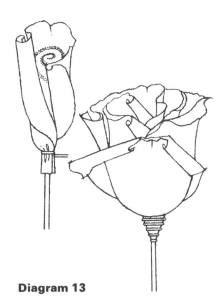

Diagram 13

Let it become tacky.

Wrap the sepals piece round the glued area. Secure tightly with one wire at base (photograph H). Curl the sepals, some upwards and some downwards to give the most natural effect.

From the green crêpe paper, cut out one central leaf and one pair of leaves for each flower.

To arrange leaves on rose buds, fold leaf in half lengthways and crease it down the centre. Place it behind a rose wire, so that the wire and the leaf overlap by about ½-inch (Diagram 14). Wrap the base of the leaf round the rose wire and tape it with floral tape three times round, horizontally. Bend over the short end of the rose wire on top of the taped strip, and tape round it two or three times (Diagram 15). Crease each leaf of the pair down the middle, and arrange the base centrally on the back of the wire, keeping them in position between the thumb and first finger. Continue taping to include them (Diagram 16). To strengthen the leaves at this point, go round three times before continuing down the stem.

To make more fully-developed roses, you can use the rose bud as the flower centre, and simply add three more petals. Cut these petals from the same pattern, and fix them in position, equally spaced around the outside of the flower. In other words, divide your imaginary clockface into three this time. You will find that these petals have to be stretched more than the rose bud ones, as they have a more bulky outline to cover. It will not be possible to keep the outer petals level and, indeed, they do not need to be. They should be a little lower than the inner four petals, as if they were curling outwards. Fix the leaves as described under rose buds. The finished flower is shown in photograph I.

The rose bud and rose patterns, with cotton wool centres, have been designed for waxing, and you will find full instructions for this in the following chapter. The flowers look very pretty just as they are, but they inevitably look like paper flowers. Waxing gives them a different translucent texture and, of course, makes them last much longer.

If you want to make coloured crêpe paper flowers for waxing, you might like to match up the cotton wool used for the centres with the colour of your flower. You can buy cotton wool balls in pale colours such as lemon, pink and blue — we used the yellow ones for the roses shown on the cover and

H

I

the pink ones for those photographed with the Victorian flower dome. Each ball of cotton wool is big enough to make two rose centres. Unravel it and divide it in two. When the cotton wool has been wrapped round the central wire you will find that it fluffs out very slightly. The best way to overcome this is to snip it with the scissors to neaten. Then follow the rest of the instructions for making roses.

We found that the single thickness of crêpe paper given for the rose leaf pattern did not take at all well to waxing. It just was not strong enough to stay in shape like doubled ones. Therefore, if you are intending to wax your flowers, stop when you have a rose bud or a fully opened rose on the flower stem and turn to the next chapter. You will find instructions for adapting the leaf pattern, another pattern for making ivy leaves for waxing, and a way of using natural ivy leaves, too.

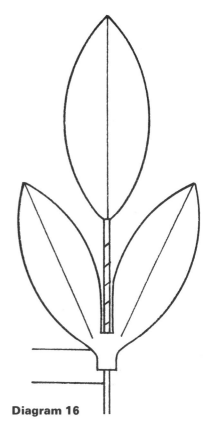

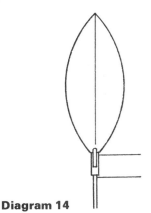

Diagram 14

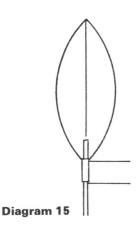

Diagram 15

Diagram 16

3 Waxed Flowers

Pretty as a picture on the cover of this book — a posy of waxed roses and 'harebells' in the glowing shades of golden yellow and mellow brown that typify a late summer evening. In the colour photograph facing page 26 we show the flowers in a different mood, this time in pinky browns, mounted on the base of a Victorian flower dome, conjuring up pictures of the cluttered family drawing rooms of times past.

Actually, this is a practical idea for displaying these nearly everlasting flowers. Houseproud mothers who worry about 'dust-traps' can relax when the flowers are protected by glass. It gives the flowers a remote and untouchable quality, and a certain mystery, too, this idea that is now coming back into favour.

And an air of mystery the flowers certainly have, for who would believe that they are simply crêpe paper roses, almost exactly the same as the ones in the preceding chapter, dipped into the melted wax of household candles?

We admit that the type of tall, elegant flower dome we used is not all that easy to come by. You might just find one in your local junk shop, or come across a similar dome that once covered a revolving pendulum clock. If not you can improvise by arranging a group of flowers in a decorative plain glass jar, one that might have held bath salts or even stem ginger. Look in the china and glass departments of large stores for huge brandy-glass shaped vases, arrange the flowers in a foam block or Plasticine on a stout piece of card and invert the glass over the top. Or make a small posy of the tiny harebell flowers and arrange them on a card to fit inside an ordinary chain store water tumbler. Tip this upside down over the flowers, and you will have a lovely miniature arrangement for your dressing table.

There is nothing complicated about the process of waxing flowers, but it is as well to accustom yourself to it before you actually start dipping in flowers which have taken you precious time to make.

. We cannot stress too strongly that waxing isn't a game for children to play. It has all the potential interest they look for in family leisure sessions — what child doesn't like something with a bit of magic about it? In goes a piece of crêpe paper and out comes a sheet of wax; in goes a limp paper flower and out comes one looking like delicate porcelain! But wax has to be heated to a very high temperature and at this stage needs careful handling. There isn't a boiling point to wax, but the danger point is around 340°F. This is when black fumes start to rise.

For waxing flowers you need to heat the wax to 310°F, or

Waxed crêpe paper Christmas roses, roses and harebells and ivy

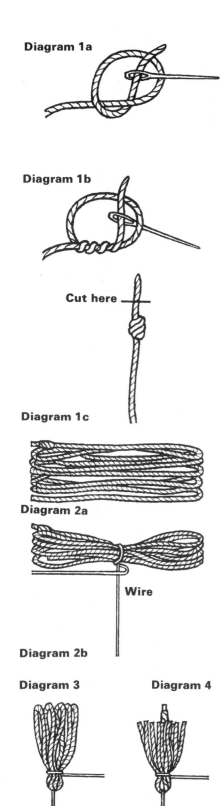

Diagram 1a

Diagram 1b

Cut here ———

Diagram 1c

Diagram 2a

Wire

Diagram 2b

Diagram 3   **Diagram 4**

a maximum of 325°F. If you are using a sweet-making thermometer, as we did, this is the point at which it usually says 'crack'. If you do not have a thermometer, the way to test the wax is to dip in a piece of crêpe paper: if a slight hissing sound occurs and minute bubbles appear, then it is right. If no bubbles are forthcoming, the wax is still not hot enough, and once a slight twist of smoke appears, it is too hot.

Ordinary household candles – the kind we all keep ready for power cuts – are the cheapest form of wax to use for this technique. For most of the work in this chapter, we used pure paraffin wax in candle form, which you can buy in economy packs from craft shops all over the country. Since candlemaking has become such a popular hobby, there has been a boom in supplies available for waxed flower making!

The wax is melted in a small completely clean saucepan. It is very important that not the slightest trace of grease or detergent remains on the surface, and the wax must be covered after use, to protect it from dust. If you can, choose a saucepan which is deep rather than wide and flat, it is more economical on the wax. The amount of wax you need will depend on the depth of the flower or leaf you are dipping into it – you need a depth of about 1½ inches for the little yellow harebells and about 3 inches for the waxed ivy and roses.

The flower heads must be finished down to the last detail before waxing. It is virtually impossible to make any last-minute adjustments after waxing without cracking the surface and completely ruining the appearance. However, you are unlikely to achieve a completely smooth surface and little excess blobs of wax can be scraped off very carefully with a fingernail.

Flowers and leaves are waxed separately. Flowers must be waxed before taping and leaves waxed before adding to the main stem.

You can wax practically any paper flowers, but not all the accessories and trimmings take so well to the process. For instance, flowers with bead or button centres are unsuitable (the wax clogs unattractively) as are the Raffene centres of the white crêpe paper star flowers in the preceding chapter. That is why we have designed a rose with a cotton wool centre, and a Christmas rose with a string centre, specially for waxing.

Crêpe paper turns several shades darker after waxing, so try to bear this in mind when choosing your colours. White crêpe paper turns a delicate cream colour, so you will not be able to match today's idea of 'brilliant whiteness' in your waxed flowers. It is better to plan your colour scheme with coloured paper and colourless wax, rather than the other way round. If you melt coloured candles, even strong coloured ones, they give a very pastel result, and sometimes a streaky one at that.

WAXED 'HAREBELL' FLOWERS

It is a good idea to make flowers of different shapes and sizes when you are planning a posy or other arrangement of waxed flowers. You can see from the colour photographs how the round, full rose shape complements the smaller, spiky outlines of the harebells and ivy and vice versa.

For each flower you will need:

Crêpe paper for petals (we used yellow, white, orange and pink); contrasting crêpe for sepals (we found that brown toned better than green); embroidery thread (not stranded cotton); needle; fine wire or rose wires; pencil; thin card for templates; tracing paper or greaseproof paper; scissors; tweezers; rubber adhesive; floral tape in colour to match sepals and leaves (ours was brown).

Make the stamens first. For the pistil, take a length from a hank of thread, without cutting it. Thread a needle and make a loop (Diagram 1(a)). Take the threaded needle through the loop ten times to form a knot (Diagram 1(b)) and then cut the thread just above the knot, as shown in Diagram 1(c). This knot becomes the pistil of the flower.

Fold the thread backwards and forwards, still without cutting, to make eight loops (including the knotted one) each measuring 2 inches long — that is, a total of 16 inches. Diagram 2(a) shows this clearly.

Holding the eight loops firmly in the middle, secure with the centre of a rose wire, twisting it round two or three times (Diagram 2(b)). With one end of the rose wire, tie the threads just above the base, wrapping the wire round so that the threads are now standing up vertically. Fasten off and cut this short length of wire (Diagram 3).

Cut the loops through a little below the pistil you have made, so that it stands up above them. (Diagram 4.)

Now you can practise waxing for the first time. Obviously, although our instructions are given for making one flower, it is advisable to make a number together and have a 'production line' for waxing in the kitchen. Hot wax splashes readily, and cold, set wax can be extremely difficult to remove from some surfaces (particularly rough surfaces) so you should cover yourself literally from head to foot with an all-enveloping apron or 'suit' of plastic wardrobe bags, and spread newspaper all around the area you will be working, even covering the walls.

Melt the wax, either household candles or paraffin wax, and heat it very slowly to 310°F (photograph A), as described at the beginning of this chapter. Dip the wired stamens (one flower at a time) into the wax, so that the wax fully covers the base. Hold in the wax while you count four, and then remove. Give the stamens several good shakes, keeping them upside-down. This is when you need yourself and the kitchen well protected. Stand the wire stem in a block of foam or something similar for two minutes, until the wax is dry. Then very carefully separate the cotton strands.

Trace the outline for the petals (Diagram 5) on to tracing paper or greaseproof paper, transfer it to thin card and cut out a template. Draw round this shape on to the crêpe paper — yellow, pink or the colour of your choice. Cut out the pattern in crêpe paper.

With the right side (matt side) facing you, carefully stretch the petal shape beneath first one pair of petals and then, on the other side, beneath the other pair (Diagram 6 shows you where the stretch is needed). Cut a slit where indicated at the

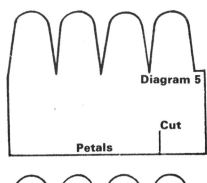

Diagram 5

Cut

Petals

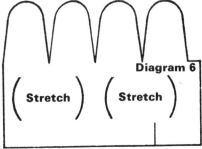

Diagram 6

(**Stretch**) (**Stretch**)

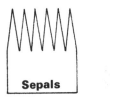

Sepals   **Diagram 7**

A

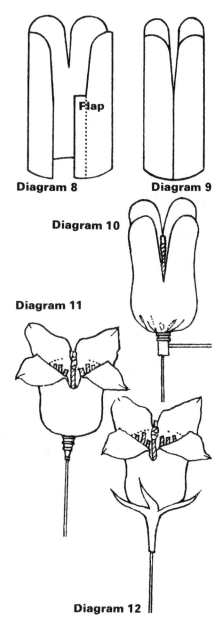

Diagram 8

Diagram 9

Diagram 10

Diagram 11

Diagram 12

B

base on the right-hand side, beneath the end petal, for the wire to pass through.

Wrap the petal piece round, underlapping the flap, as indicated in Diagram 8. Use rubber adhesive to glue the flap. Self-adhesive tape would be unsuitable in this case, as it melts in wax. The petal piece forms a cylinder as shown in Diagram 9.

Slip petals from the bottom up the stem, allowing binding wire to come through the slit you have cut. Compress the edges at the base, gathering up the paper rather as you would the waistline of a skirt, and tie the wire round about three or four times (Diagram 10). With you finger gently push out any creases and fill out the 'bulges' you stretch in the petals. Continue doing this all the way round until the flower is a good shape.

Curl over petals to make a bell-shaped flower (Diagram 11). Give each a pinch between finger and thumb to crease it lengthways. Wire the petals neatly round the base. Separate the stamens and curl over with tweezers. Arrange the pistil centrally. Cut out the sepals (Diagram 7) from brown crêpe paper. Spread the glue sparingly around the petal base and on the inside of the sepals. Allow it to become tacky and then stick sepals in position, as shown in photograph B and in Diagram 12. They will probably not need wiring.

The flower is now ready to be waxed. Reheat the wax to 310°F, as before, and dip each flower quickly in and out. Shake the flower vigorously upside-down to remove excess wax and stand, not touching other flowers, to dry. Do not leave the flowers near the heat.

When the flower is dry, tape it as described, using floral tape in a colour to match the sepals and leaves. As ours were brown, we chose brown floral tape. Photograph B shows two views of the finished flower, after waxing.

ROSE LEAVES FOR WAXING

In the previous chapter, we explained that the rose leaf pattern would not be completely suitable for waxing. If, therefore, you have made some roses for waxing, follow these instructions for the leaves.

You will need:

Crêpe paper (either olive green or brown); picture wire; rubber adhesive; pencil; tracing paper or greaseproof paper; thin card for template; sharp scissors and nail scissors; equipment for waxing as described.

Decide how many leaves you want for each flower — you can use the central one alone, or three on each stem. Cut out the leaf patterns (Diagram 13, page 32) twice, from crêpe paper; you want to use them double thickness for waxing.

Cut a length of picture wire for each leaf, about 5–6 inches long. Dip the wire in rubber adhesive for the length of the leaf and lay it flat on the leaf pattern from just below the tip to the base. Lay the other leaf pattern on top of the wire, carefully matching the edges with those of the pattern below (Diagram 14). Weight the leaf down with a coin and leave for about half an hour to dry. You will find that the wire in the centre gives a realistic vein effect and is a great improvement to the design.

Elegant paeony flowers in starched organdie and lawn

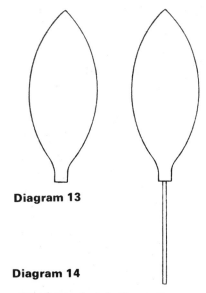

Diagram 13

Diagram 14

C

Still anxious for authenticity? With a small pair of nail scissors, snip little notches out of the pattern, starting at the top, all the way down both sides of the leaf, with the tiny points going upwards (see photograph C). Curl each leaf very slightly at the top.

Wax each leaf separately, following the general instructions for waxing already given. Shake the excess wax from the leaf and then press the top together quickly, to seal if necessary.

Tape each leaf separately. You can use either floral tape or crêpe paper strip in the same colour as the leaf. Since the floral tape has a slightly shiny, waxen look already, it seems to look less obtrusive than unwaxed crêpe paper. (Because of the length of the stems, it takes a lot of wax to coat the crêpe-covered wires.) Bind the leaves to form a spray (photograph D).

Fix the leaf or leaves on to the stem of the rose, as shown in photograph E.

WAXED PAPER IVY LEAVES
Just as you would with natural flowers, you will find that with paper or waxed flower arrangements, it is useful to have some separate leaves, other than those wired to the flowers, to extend the height or width of the outline and to provide a contrast in shape, texture and colour. The extra leaves can contribute enormously to the overall effect.

For the ivy leaves you will need:
Brown wrapping paper — the kind with a very narrow shiny self-stripe (or you could buy the same quality in green, mauve or other colours); 20-gauge picture wire; rubber adhesive; 'natural'-coloured floral tape; pencil; tracing or greaseproof paper; thin card for template; scissors. Equipment for waxing.

Trace the patterns given on this page (Diagram 15) for each of the four leaves, reverse the tracings on to a piece of card and draw over the outlines with a soft pencil. Cut out the card templates. Double the paper, and then draw round the templates. Cut through both thicknesses of paper for each leaf.

Cut lengths of picture wire from between about 4 inches for the longest leaves to 2 inches for the smallest. Straighten the

Diagram 15

32

wires. Set out the leaves in pairs to avoid confusion.

Dip a length of the picture wire into the rubber adhesive, gluing it for the length of the leaf. Lay the wire on one leaf pattern, from just below the tip of the leaf, straight down the centre (Diagram 16). Weight down with a coin and leave for the glue to dry. This takes about half an hour.

With a small strand of wire, press 'vein' marks from the centre of the leaf out towards the 'points' of the leaf pattern, four times for the two largest leaves, twice for the medium-sized leaf, but not for the smallest one (Diagram 17). Bend the wire stalk almost to a right-angle and slightly bend the tip of the leaf up or down. The wire centre will ensure that the leaf holds this shape (photograph F). Wax each leaf separately, as already described, and shake well to remove excess wax.

Using floral tape, bind the stems from the bottom up — see photograph G (this is the only case in which you are recommended to start at this end) and finish by snapping off the tape underneath the turned over leaf.

Arrange the leaves into a bunch, binding the smaller ones to the stem of the larger one, or bind the individual leaves vertically on to the main stem if you want to give the arrangement the effect of a natural piece of trailing ivy. Tape each ivy leaf stem and then the main stem. Twist the wire over, say, a pencil, to give it gentle curves. Photograph H shows you a spray of waxed paper ivy leaves.

WAXED NATURAL IVY LEAVES

From paper ivy leaves to real ones. We experimented with waxing sprays of ivy leaves picked from a garden wall in the middle of the winter, and found that it worked! That is to say that, quickly dipped in and out of the hot wax, the leaves responded surprisingly well. They did not melt, disintegrate, discolour or behave in any other way than to emerge looking slightly shinier, slightly waxier, and surely longer lasting.

WAXED FLOWER PICTURE

Once you have made and waxed the flowers and leaves, you will start thinking of ways to use them decoratively in the house. Because the flowers are rather delicate and an accidental

D

E

F

G

H

Diagram 16

Diagram 17

knock might crack the wax, it is best to plan a degree of protection for your arrangements.

The photograph on page 35 shows a deep picture frame, which we had made specially for the purpose, covered with velvet to display a posy of roses and the 'harebell' flowers. You can copy the idea with a shallower frame, covering the backing with fabric; you will realise, of course, that you would have to settle for omitting the glass. Or you can make a simple box frame by covering a liqueur chocolate box, or even a shallow wooden filing tray with fabric.

Arrange the flowers and leaves, if you choose to include some, into a posy or a spray, curling and bending the stalks so that you achieve a natural, graceful shape. Cut the stems off to a uniform length, twist a wire round to hold them in position, then bind them with a tape which will least show up against your background colour. We chose brown, because our picture frame is covered with brown velvet.

You can sew the stem on to the fabric backing, taking stitches firmly round the stem at short intervals all the way up, but this might cause a strain to be put on the background and make it pucker noticeably.

The best way to attach the flowers is to put a large dab of strong adhesive on the velvet, having checked carefully first just where the stems and the flowers will touch. Wait a few minutes for it to become tacky, then press the spray firmly into it. Weight the stem with a heavy stone while the adhesive sets.

Just for fun, and for extra colour, we pinned two summery butterflies to our arrangement. It looks as if they think the flowers are real!

VICTORIAN DOME

At the beginning of this chapter, we described other ways of protecting your waxed flowers under glass – in a Victorian dome, in upturned tumblers and so on.

To follow the glass dome arrangement, in the colour photograph facing page 26, you will need to collect some natural materials from a country walk, or buy them from a good florist.

To give height to the setting, you will need a dried root, or some thick twigs or branches, or one or two interesting pieces of dried bark or driftwood – the more gnarled and faded they are, the better – and some moss or Sphagnum moss.

For the dome arrangement you will need:

Old glass dome, or other glass container, as described; waxed flowers – the photograph shows Christmas roses, harebells, roses, paper ivy leaves and rose leaves; dried moss (Sphagnum); dried heather or dried grasses; dried root, bark or branches; foam (Styrofoam) block slightly smaller than circumference of dome base; Plasticine; garden wire.

Fix the foam firmly to the base of the dome by pushing it well down into a bed of Plasticine, or a screwed-up strip of extra-adhesive tape (Oasis-fix). Do not try to use a strong adhesive, as it will damage the foam.

Trim the root or bark, if necessary, breaking off outside pieces so that you can jam it into the foam ring. Wrap the garden wire several times round the root first, then round the ring, round the root and round the other side of the ring, over and over again until it is quite secure. Push the root firmly into the base.

Spread a thick layer of Plasticine round the outside of the foam ring, between that and the edge of the dome base — about $\frac{1}{2}$-inch. This will help you to build up the mossy layer and fix the flowers at 'ground level'.

Press a layer of moss over the root, the foam ring and the Plasticine. Build up more moss into little mounds to give a natural hillocky appearance, and to help you raise the height of the flowers.

Place the lower flowers first, arranging them so that some of the larger ones can be seen from all sides. As this is an 'all-round' arrangement, you will have to keep turning it round as you work, to make sure that it is interesting from all points of view.

Press leaves into the mossy base and through into Plasticine round the rim of the base, and others amongst the flowers, higher up.

You will need extra long stems for the climbing roses. These are twisted round the root, some on one side and some on the other, so that they form, in effect, a rose spiral. Twist ivy and rose leaves between them. Twist wire round some of the pieces of dried heather and bind them round the top of the root, and press more sprigs into the middle and lower levels of the arrangement.

4 Starched Fabric Flowers

In both fashion and interior decorating, there will always be a place for flowers made from fabric. They can be made huge and floppy or small and dainty, in materials to match curtains and covers, dress and hat. Or they can be made not as part of a team, but just for what they are — a soft and pretty decoration with an endless variety of colour and design possibilities.

In this section we show pale cream starched lawn and organdie flowers which were inspired by a photograph of paeonies — and then went their own way, design-wise. Primroses provided the germ of the idea for the flowers made up in little posies to decorate the child's boater — but then whoever heard of primroses with flowers on? These are cut from starched, flower-sprigged lawn and ring a hat that any little girl or her mother would love to have an excuse to wear. Then, with an almost film-Western influence, there are large droopy flowers in checked gingham. It was difficult to decide whether to show one pinned at the throat of a white frilly blouse or tucked into the belt of a pair of faded jeans. Make two and you could do both.

CREAM PAEONY FLOWERS
As you can see from the colour photograph facing page 30, we chose to show the flowers in an elegant table setting, surrounding a candlestick and snuffer — an attractive idea by any standard. This decoration on an occasional table, a dressing table or at dinner, would be pretty enough by itself. But, to give you other ideas, we show one flower spilling out of a silvered wine goblet — a wine glass would do equally well; flatter each guest with one beside her plate. For tea on Sundays, when there are no goblets or glasses around, a flower set on a table napkin shows extra thoughtfulness.

The soft creamy colouring of this flower makes it a perfect accessory for weddings. On a wedding cake, one flower or a group of three in a goblet would sound a triumphant note. And, for a bride's bouquet, a small, tight posy of the flowers, with perhaps two or three wired and cascading down below it: what could be prettier?

We think this kind of flower looks at its best in gentle colours. You could try very pale and not-quite-so-pale pink; two nearly matching shades of blue or, for an effect a little further from Nature, two soft shades of green. The middles are made out of combed-out sisal; you would, in this case, probably like to dye the string in a pale, toning shade.

Each flower has four petals in lawn, and eight petals and a fringed sepal in starched organdie. Once starched, the fabric is easy to cut out and handle without fraying.

You can make this type of flower from any close-weave cotton fabric, such as lawn, gingham, muslin, poplin, organdie. Open-weave fabrics would fray badly, giving an untidy appearance, and an irregular design.

For each flower you will need:

Nearly-white organdie; cream-coloured lawn (or other colours of your choice); sisal from which to cut 6 lengths of $3\frac{1}{4}$ inches; 7-inch rose wires (30 SWG); heavier wire (such as pvc-covered garden wire or 7-inch × 20g 'florist's wire'); white floral tape; starch (see directions below); rubber adhesive.

We used spray starch, holding the aerosol can about 8 inches away from the fabric, then left the starch to 'settle' for a few seconds before ironing. If using powdered starch the 'recipe' is this: mix 2 level tablespoons powdered starch to a paste with a little cold water, and add $\frac{1}{2}$ pint of boiling water. Stir, and leave to cool a little. Then dip the fabric in, stir round for a minute or two and squeeze out the excess liquid. Iron the fabric straight away. Starch and press the fabrics before you cut out the shapes. You will find the material is much easier to handle and far less likely to fray and stretch. The organdie needs starching only once, but all the other cottons mentioned need two applications, and ironing after each.

Trace the petal and the sepal shapes from the patterns on this page (Diagram 1), and transfer the outlines on to plain white card, such as an old postcard. Cut out this 'master pattern' or template.

The most reliable way to cut the shapes accurately from the fabric is to stick the template with double-sided sticky tape to the fabric, draw round the outline, peel it off, and repeat for the number of times you need to cut out the shape. However, if you find this laborious, and think you can hold it firmly with your left (or non-writing) hand without letting it slip at all, do it that way.

Pin the starched fabrics on to an old table or board, stick or hold the template in position and draw round it. You will need to draw the petal shape four times on the lawn and eight times on the organdie, and the sepal shape once on the organdie. Using very sharp scissors to eliminate the risk of snagging the fabric, cut round the outlines.

You will find that the organdie petals curl naturally as you cut them out. Do not worry. This is exactly what you want them to do. The lawn petals will not curl. You could put a gentle curl in the top, using an orange stick or hair curling pin, but it is not really necessary to take the risk of encouraging fraying.

Dab a little rubber adhesive on the base of the lawn petals and the base of the organdie petals on the side opposite to that in which they are curled. In other words, you will place the petals with the curl outwards and you want to glue the inner side. Leave the petals separately on a piece of clean white paper for about five minutes while the glue partly sets.

Bunch the six $3\frac{1}{4}$-inch lengths of sisal together. Hook a length of florist's wire over the centre and loop it round underneath so that it holds the strands firmly together (photograph A). This wire forms the top part of the stem. Pull the

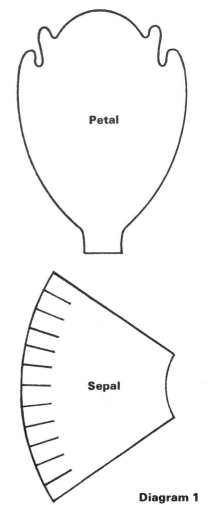

Petal

Sepal

Diagram 1

A

B

Diagram 2

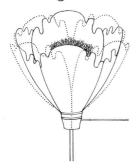

Diagram 3

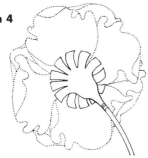

Diagram 4

ends of the sisal together to meet at the top and bind them with a length of rose wire, $\frac{1}{2}$-inch from the base.

Using a strong comb, comb the ends together until each strand is separated and they are thick and fluffy. You will find that the appearance of the string alters completely and takes on quite a new personality — that of the centre of your paeony (see photograph B). Then cut carefully into a slightly bush shape so that the top is higher than the sides — in silhouette, this now looks like a dome.

Stick two central, lawn petals $\frac{1}{2}$-inch from the sisal base, opposite each other. Tie in with rose wire. Now place remaining two central petals opposite each other and wire in position (Diagram 2). The dab of glue is to secure them temporarily while you do this, but should not be relied upon to hold them into a tight, neat shape. You will find that the dome of sisal pushes these four central petals out into the shape you want, a shallow cone.

Continue by positioning the outer, organdie petals, placing them so that they curl outwards. The first circle of four organdie petals should fill in the gaps between the four lawn petals (see Diagram 3) with the last four alternated between them. Bind tightly with a rose wire.

With the white floral tape, bind over the 'calyx', covering the rose wires and just coming over the top of the stem. This hides any slightly rough edges of the petals.

Make cuts in the sepal pieces as indicated by the lines on the pattern, so that the top curve is fringed. This will enable it to 'fan out' to take up the width and space of the petals beneath it. As with all types of artificial flowers, it is important to achieve a neat finish at this point. A lumpy 'calyx' beneath the petals makes the flower look clumsy and unattractive.

Fit the sepal pieces over the calyx so that the fringed edge goes over the floral tape and the narrow base just covers the top of the stem. Secure with a rose wire about $\frac{1}{4}$-inch from base.

You might find it easier to fix and wire the sepal piece if the flower is balanced upside down (Diagram 4), either on a flat base or in a shallow cup, leaving you both hands free to work. Do not try to cut corners or make a more secure job of this part of the operation by gluing the sepals to the calyx. Remember that organdie is very fine material, and the glue would show through.

Wind white floral tape over the stem, starting at the base of the calyx with two or three horizontal winds and then working down the stem diagonally, as already described. You should now have a flower that looks like the one in the close-up photographs C1 and C2.

PRIMROSE POSY

The decoration on the child's boater, shown in the colour photograph facing page 50, is made up of a number of posies, each one a cluster of tiny 'primroses' cut from starched plain and floral-sprigged Liberty lawn. If you have a hat which needs decoration, but not as much as this, one or two of these posies pushed under the band could work wonders on a bright spring day. Or you could use a posy as a buttonhole — certainly cheaper than buying yourself a corsage, and these flowers won't wilt. They will look as fresh and pretty at dusk as they did at dawn.

If you are a dressmaker, and are making yourself an outfit in any of the light cotton fabrics recommended for this type of flower, it is a good idea to make a posy or two to match the dress and wear it on a plain belt or sewn or pinned to your handbag. Little touches of this kind are what is meant by the 'couture look'.

As you can see from the close-up photographs of the posies (D, E and F), they are made with alternative leaf formations — when you are not sticking entirely to the botany book, you can please yourself to just that small extent.

One posy (D) has a group of three leaves with serrated edges — one large one in the middle and a smaller one on either side. The other version (E and F) has one slightly larger leaf, creased down the centre and making a 'cup' for the primrose flowers.

Since some of the prettiest spring posies are a nosegay of flowers in different colours, you can introduce a little variety into yours, too, and delve deep into the pieces bag. Make some of the five-petalled shapes from patterned material, with plain, fringed centres to contrast. And reverse the process for others — make some plain flowers with patterned centres.

For these flowers, you can use sea-island cotton, cotton lawn, organdie, voile, gingham, poplin — any cotton, in fact, with a fairly close weave. Starch all fabrics except organdie twice, in the way described for the 'paeony' flowers, above. In the case of organdie, you need to starch only once.

Each posy has five or six flowers. Each flower consists of a five-petal shape; a choice of one large or a group of three leaves made from green cotton; a fringed cotton centre and either a single bead or a group of five small ones. The wire stems are bound with green floral tape.

For each posy you will need:

1 packet rose wires (7-inch × 30 SWG); small beads or larger beads, bought in a packet of assorted colours; floral tape; cotton fabric as described for the petals, stamens and leaves; spray starch or powdered starch; pencil; tracing paper or greaseproof paper; thin card for the templates; scissors; serrated-edged scissors if available.

Sort out the fabrics into the three types you will need — floral-sprigged and plain for the flowers, and plain dark or light green for the leaves. Starch the fabric in the piece, before cutting out, giving all cottons other than organdie two applications, and ironing after each, and organdie only one.

Trace the pattern shapes from Diagram 5 on page 40. Transfer the tracings on to plain white card (old postcards will do well) and cut out the templates very accurately.

Pin each fabric to a flat surface to keep it in place; stick each template to the appropriate fabric with double-sided sticky tape (or hold it with your left hand so that it doesn't move even the tiniest fraction of an inch) and draw round with a pencil.

Unpin the fabrics and cut out the shapes, using ordinary dressmaking scissors for the two flower pieces and the large, single leaf, and, for a natural effect, serrated scissors can be used

D

E

F

Diagram 5

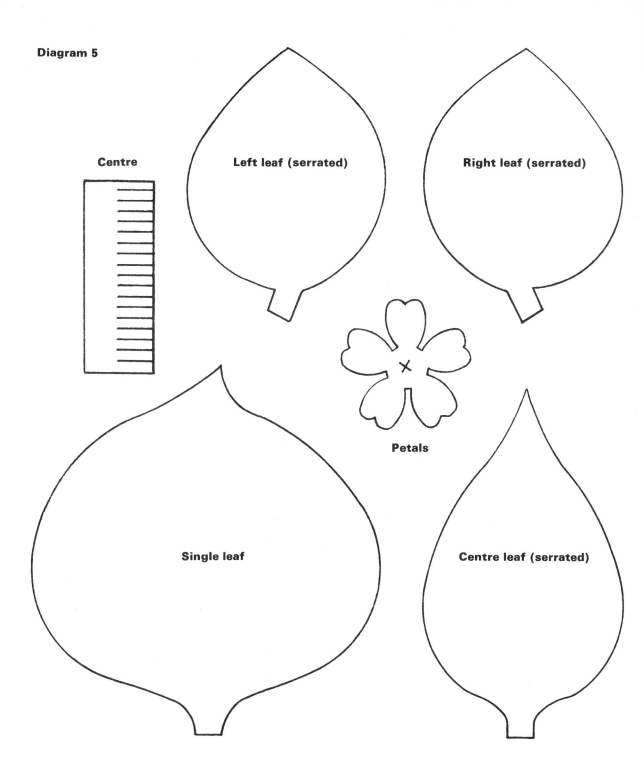

Centre

Left leaf (serrated)

Right leaf (serrated)

Petals

Single leaf

Centre leaf (serrated)

(if available) for the group of three leaves.

To each flower, take a 7-inch length of rose wire and push either one large bead or five small ones half-way along it (see photograph G). Twist the wire a few times to secure.

Make cuts as indicated by the lines drawn on the pattern, along the fabric strip for the flower centre. Wrap this round the centre, just covering the beads (see photograph H). Wire this in position and fasten off the wire. The strip must be held tightly at the bottom and will fan out at the top. Cut a small cross in the middle of the five-petalled shape, where indicated on the diagram (don't make too large a cut) and push this up on to the wire.

Bind the flower with green floral tape, starting horizontally at the top (calyx) and then working diagonally down the stem (see photograph I). With these very small flowers, you will find it necessary to work extra carefully and neatly at this stage.

Make five or six flowers in a similar way for each posy. Arrange the flowers at different heights into an attractive bunch. Cut the stems off so that they are level. Secure them together with a rose wire where the leaf is to go, giving the wire three or four twists (see photograph J). Leave the other end of the wire free to fix on the leaf or leaves.

Fold the single leaf lengthwise down the centre, making the crease with your fingernail (which is easy to do on starched fabric) or ironing it. Wire it in position (see detail in photograph F).

When using the group of three serrated leaves, fix the centre leaf in place first, behind the flower stems, then the other two, one on either side (see photograph D). The little 'stalk' of each of these side leaves is designed to lean in towards the centre, so be sure to fix the leaves on the appropriate side of the central one. Bind over wire. Snip stalks to required length and bind down to the bottom.

CHECKED GINGHAM FLOWERS

Woven checked cotton always looks crisp and summery, and it's so versatile and useful that it never goes out of fashion. Because it is cheap and durable, too, it is a good choice for large areas. Not everyone has the patience to cover their walls with it – though we know one house where, in large brown and white checks, it looks stunning – but there must be thousands of homes where it is used for curtains. Think how pretty it would look if you have a bedroom or living room with gingham furnishings, to have a bunch of these floppy flowers, either standing in a vase or, better still, mounted in an old frame to make a picture. You could chose the same colour but, because of the scale of the items, a different size of check. And, once you gain confidence, you could easily adapt the pattern to make your flowers slightly larger than the ones we show, which measure $4\frac{1}{2}$ inches across. The larger the flowers are, the more they will droop, of course – but this could be part of their charm.

Then, as we have said, these flowers have other possibilities. They look great tucked into the neck of a blouse, pinned high on the shoulder or on a bag or belt. A hat with a broad, sweeping brim could take one at the side and a long, swirling summer

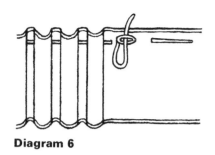

Diagram 6

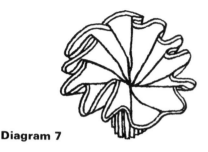

Diagram 7

skirt could take several around the hem. Instant party wear! In fact, if we don't stop giving you ideas, you'll have to go into mass production!

For each flower you will need:

12 inches of 1-inch-wide ribbon or cheap cotton tape (we used black); needle; thread to match tape; 1 length of pvc-covered wire for stem; 9 inches fine wire for binding; plain cotton fabric for centre and underneath base; contrasting (gingham) material for two rounds of petals; pencil; tracing paper or greaseproof paper; thin card for templates; scissors; bouclé wool or tape or matching fabric to bind stems; starch (either spray or powder); fabric adhesive.

Knot the thread firmly into the tape or ribbon and take small running stitches along one edge (Diagram 6). Pull the free end of the thread as tightly as you can to gather the tape into a rosette. Backstitch a few times to secure it. Break off thread (Diagram 7).

Make a loop at the top of the stem wire so that it won't fall through, and push it down through the centre of the rosette until the loop is obscured in the folds (Diagram 8).

Take the wire and twist it two or three times round the rosette $\frac{1}{4}$-inch from the bottom to secure it. (Diagram 9).

Starch both the plain and gingham fabrics twice, ironing after each application. The way to do this is described fully under the instructions for making the organdie paeony flowers.

Diagram 8

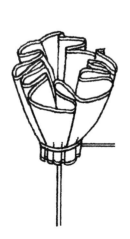

Diagram 9

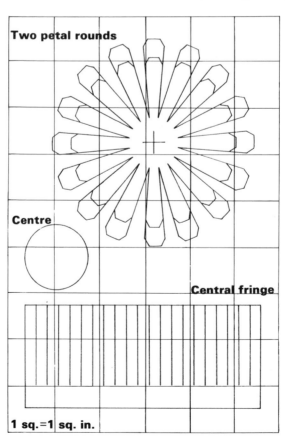

Two petal rounds

Centre

Central fringe

1 sq.=1 sq. in.

Diagram 10

42

Transfer the patterns for the two petal-rounds (notice that one has a shorter diameter than the other), the base and the centre (Diagram 10) on to white card and cut out templates.

Using these templates as already described, cut out the larger petal-round from the starched gingham and the smaller petal-round and the base piece from the plain cotton.

Cross cut on each of the petals where indicated on the pattern to give almost pointed ends. Cut narrow slits, to within $\frac{1}{2}$-inch of the bottom, all along the centre piece, as shown by the lines on the pattern. There is no need to trace these lines in — you will easily be able to cut them free-hand.

Wrap central fringe around rosette and tie with wire; position it so that the fringe starts where the wire has been tied previously. Finish off wire by binding tightly over base of fringe, as you will have no further use for this wire (see photograph K).

Glue the base to the part of the flower already made *just above* the wire. Ease on the smaller layer of petals above the wire. Glue again just underneath where the petals are, ease on second layer of petals. See that both layers are pushed up over the wire, as in the photograph.

Glue an area about 1 inch across on the second layer of petals *around the stem* and ease on the base (photograph L).

You can finish these flowers with tape or bouclé wool, if you prefer (see photograph M), but for the most decorative finish, we used a strip of the gingham fabric. On the bias (cross) of the fabric, cut a long strip $\frac{1}{2}$-inch wide. Fold in half, to give you a double strip $\frac{1}{4}$-inch wide and iron it to make the strip as flat as possible.

Put a dab of glue on one end of the fabric, and press it in place immediately under the circular base of the flower, making a start on the 'calyx'. Wind it round horizontally two or three times, then start working diagonally down the stem, making sure that you overlap the binding well to give a completely all-over effect. Finish off at the bottom end with a dab of glue and leave to dry.

5 Stained Glass Window Flowers

Someone once said of a photographer that he paints with light. So do other artists, when one thinks about it. The beautiful stained glass windows one can see in country churches and city cathedrals 'paint' intricate, kaleidoscopic patterns on the walls as the sun slants through the colours. In this chapter, we tried to bring this effect right down to earth by making flower and snowflake patterns covered with layer upon layer of different coloured Cellophane paper. As you can see from the colour photograph facing page 54, these decorations do a great deal to brighten a grey rooftop scene.

As one becomes more ambitious, other shapes and patterns could be created. At Christmas time, for instance, there is endless scope to make decorations with a Nativity theme, a Christmas tree shape with a lighted candle effect, and so on. At Easter, children would enjoy making a hen and chick scene, and this method could be used for a colourful birthday card.

Flower shapes like ours are easy to make, and employ that popular primary school craft, paper cutting. The designs use matt black paper, folded and cut into shapes to resemble the lead strips between pieces of stained glass. Any paper will do, so long as it does not let the light through. And the colours in between are the results of experiment, with one colour after another added as if it were paint in an artist's palette.

By using just the primary colours of red, yellow and blue, in different mixtures, you can make all the secondary colours — purple, orange and green — to any depth you like. The more layers of paper you use, the more intense will be the colour. For instance, two layers of red and two layers of yellow will make something very intense; one layer of each colour would admit more light and apparently weaken the colour. You will find that you can create an enormous range of pinky mauves, bluey mauves, deep purple and beetroot colours with just the blue and red papers. Hold them up to a window or an electric light to see what effect you are obtaining before sticking them in place.

You can use tissue paper instead of Cellophane, and you might well be tempted to do so because it comes in a far wider range of colours. However, you will have to take particular care because it tears more easily; and, let's face it, it isn't nearly as shiny and stained-glass-window-looking as Cellophane.

For the best effects, either stick the paper-covered shapes on to a window in an attractive group which enhances the view outside, as we have done, or cut a second paper shape, stick it on the back to neaten and string each decoration at different levels to make a mobile. Hang this in front of an electric light — though not too near the bulb or the paper will discolour and may even catch fire.

For each silhouette you will need:

Matt black or other dark-coloured paper, or thick golden foil, or foil-covered paper (see directions); assortment of colours of Cellophane or tissue paper; pair of compasses it available; pencil; sharp scissors; tracing paper or greaseproof paper; transparent self-adhesive tape and double-sided adhesive tape (Sellotape).

There are four patterns for the outlines shown in the colour photograph. You can see each one clearly in the silhouette pictures on page 46. Patterns 1 and 2 are cut from 7-inch diameter circles folded into three, to give one-eighth sections. Pattern 3, another 7-inch diameter circle, is folded only twice and cut from a quarter-circle segment. Pattern 4 has a diameter of $11\frac{3}{4}$ inches and is cut after folding three times, into eighths.

For a glistening-all-over effect, we show Pattern 2 cut from the heavy-weight golden foil, which is ideal for Christmas decorations. You can, in fact, use this material for all the shapes, but it is best to practise first with the matt black paper. The foil is more difficult to cut accurately and slightly temperamental when you want it to keep still or stay flat! It does repay the extra care, though. You can see that our Pattern 2 looks as bright and shiny as the rising sun itself.

Trace the outlines of the designs from the patterns. In this case, there is no need to cut a card template. You can transfer the shapes from the tracing paper direct. With a pair of compasses, or using a plate or a record of suitable size, draw the circles as already described on to the black or foil paper and cut them out. Fold the paper circles twice or three times, as indicated, and transfer the traced outlines on to the quarter or eighth-circle segment. To do this, reverse the tracing paper, pencilled side down, and go over the outline again in pencil.

Using very sharp scissors and holding the paper shape very carefully, begin by cutting away the outline. You will find it easier to do this accurately if you use short, snipping movements with the scissors rather than attempt to do it in long sweeping lines all at once. If the layers of paper appear to be slipping, paper-clip the side you are holding for extra firmness.

You will find that all the cut-out areas can be accomplished quite simply from the folded-over edges. The only exception is in Pattern 3. To cut out the four small circle shapes, you need to cut out all the side pieces and then fold the paper pattern over again; follow the lines indicating 'fold'. Then cut out a semi-circle.

After cutting out the shapes, open each one up very carefully to avoid tearing. You can see the outlines of the silhouettes clearly in pictures A, B, C and D. Lay each piece on a flat surface and press it with heavy weights, or place between some large books to 'iron out' the creases.

While the paper shapes are being flattened, you can begin your experiments with colour. It is easiest if you cut some sheets of the Cellophane paper into quarters, and then try mixing them one on top of the other until you find a number of effects you like. Although complete contrasts can be quite striking, variations on a one-colour theme are often the most pleasing.

Just for guidance, here are the colours used in our patterns.
Pattern 1, photograph A: one layer pink, 1 blue; 1 layer pink,

Pattern 1

Pattern 2

Pattern 3

Pattern 4

2 blue; 1 layer pink, 3 layers blue; 2 layers pink, 1 layer blue; 1 layer pink; 2 layers pink; 2 layers pink, 1 layer yellow; 1 layer pink, 2 layers yellow.

Pattern 2, photograph B: 1 layer yellow and 2 layers blue.

Pattern 3, photograph C: Complete layer of yellow; pink circle covering four inner 'triangles'; scraps of blue and extra yellow on four outside 'triangles' and scraps of extra pink and extra yellow on four circles.

Pattern 4, photograph D: Inner circle of blue; outer ring of yellow; four pink 'hearts' covering alternate segments; complete layer of pink over all.

When you have decided which colours you want to use, put the tracing of the paper shape on to the Cellophane or tissue paper, and follow the outline with a pencil. For best results, use an H pencil for cellophane and HB or B for tissue paper. The indentation will show through quite clearly enough for you to follow.

Have ready several small strips of sticky tape, about $\frac{1}{4}$-inch long. Stick them separately on to the back of your hand. Place each piece of coloured paper in position, on the wrong side of the paper shape, and secure with sticky tape. In order to follow your pre-determined colour plan, it is probably easiest to make a rough sketch of the paper shape and pencil in the colours you are going to use, for instance red; red and orange; orange and yellow; and so on all the way round all the segments.

It goes without saying that decorations as eye-catching as these will focus attention on your windows, so make sure that the glass is clean before you put them in position. Fix them to the glass with double-sided self-adhesive tape (Sellotape). You will find that lighting effects are particularly good in early morning and late afternoon. And, as it happens, these are the times of day when many photographers find that they achieve the best lighting effects, too.

C

A

B

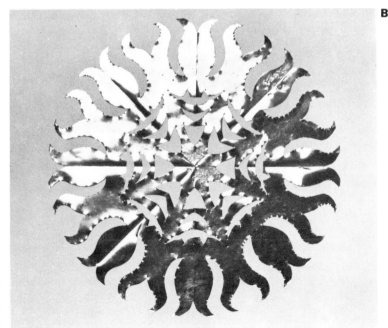

D

47

6 Nearly-Natural Flowers

You can't improve on Nature, everyone knows that. But, by developing an awareness of the possibilities, you can make flowers that look nearly natural from materials that might otherwise be wasted. The lovely chestnut-brown beech masts, with their creamy velvety centres, might so easily be crushed underfoot on an autumn walk; here, they ring a seed pod (rescued from the bonfire?) to make a 'flower' that will last for ever. Cones, sometimes so difficult to use by themselves, are outlined with those glistening, papery honesty seed heads; the brown and silver flowers make attractive Christmas decorations, as they are, or you could spray them with silver or gold paint.

Honesty must be one of the most versatile of all the 'everlastings' we can grow in our gardens. And, luckily, it needs little encouragement. Indeed some serious gardeners who have remained unenlightened about its potential as a floral art material, have been known unfeelingly to refer to it as 'they weeds'!

Firstly, we show the honesty 'petals' surrounding a single, fully opened fir cone (illustration A). The honesty makes a ring round the cone, like hazy moonshine. For clarity, we show the 'flower' with only one row of honesty petals, but you can build up several layers, using honesty of diminishing sizes, until only the tip of the cone shows.

To begin, you will need to wire the cone. Use a 7-inch rose wire, twist it two or three times round the first row of 'petals' on the cone, bring the short end close to the base of the cone and twist it firmly round the long end (see Diagram 1). Using a clear adhesive (such as Bostik) sparingly on a matchstick or orange stick, put a dab at the base of each honesty 'petal' and push it between two woody layers of the cone. The size of the cone will determine how many honesty petals you will use in the first row — between five and seven gives a pretty shape. If you build up more layers of honesty, position the next row of petals in between those in the first row, and so on.

Bind the stem with a narrow ($\frac{1}{4}$-inch) strip of brown crêpe paper or with brown floral tape, working from the top and, in the case of the crêpe, starting and finishing with a dab of glue.

Illustration B shows another way of using honesty, this time surrounding a delicate papery seed pod, from a 'Shoo-Fly' plant. The whole effect is ethereal. First of all, wire the seed head with a 7-inch rose wire, pushing the wire carefully through from underneath, bringing it across the base of the pod, and back through the other side. Twist the short end of wire round the one you will use for the stem. This time, you start with the inner layers of honesty petals sticking them with clear adhesive to the underside of the seed pod; four petals will probably be enough. Make sure they are firmly in place, and then continue by. sticking to them the five petals that form the next row; six after that, and possibly finishing with a fourth row of seven petals. Be very sparing with the glue. The petals are very light, they will not come under pressure, and you do not want to spoil the appearance of the flower with ugly smears.

When the glue is dry on all the layers, bind the stem with white floral tape.

These flowers look particularly charming in candlelight. You could stick a row of these flowers close together all round a small foam ring and stand a candle in the centre. Another way to show them at their romantic best is to stick them into a foam ball, again close together so that the foam surface is fully covered, and hang it where it will catch the light. One of these flowers pinned on to a simple velvet-ribbon napkin ring for each guest at Christmas time, transforms a table and is prettier than most Christmas crackers.

From an all-silvery look to a midnight-blue effect. The next flower, illustration C, page 50, has a centre cluster of blueberry-coloured ivy seed pods. These, as small and tight as a packet of wooden beads, make a most striking centre to a circle of honesty petals. The seed heads are wired on the stalk, the honesty stuck on to the under side of the cluster, and the stem bound with white floral tape. See the flower, in all its glory, in the candle arrangement, page 52.

Beech masts take on a new lease of life in the flower shown in illustration D. The pod forming the centre of the flower is from a tree paeony, but you could use an iris pod, or any other of a similar shape and proportion. Wire the pod and then each of the five beechmasts with rose wires, then twist all the wires together to form one stem. It is important to do this as tightly as possible to get a neat finish. Bind the stem with brown crêpe paper or brown floral tape. That's all!

Another way to use beech masts decoratively (illustration E) is to take a fully-opened specimen and give it a colourful centre. In the example we chose, an orangey-coral helichrysum, the two went so well together that they really did look as if they had grown that way. To do this you will need to wire the helichrysum flower as soon as it is picked, not leave it until it is dry and brittle. It is a good idea to wire a bunch of these flowers all at once, as they have so many uses in flower decoration and flower making.

Pierce a hole through the bottom of the beech mast, using a strong darning needle and a thimble, since the material is tough and woody. Poke the wire through, from the top, so that the flower nestles in the centre. Bind the stem as before, using brown crêpe or floral tape.

Sometimes on a woodland walk you will find fir cones

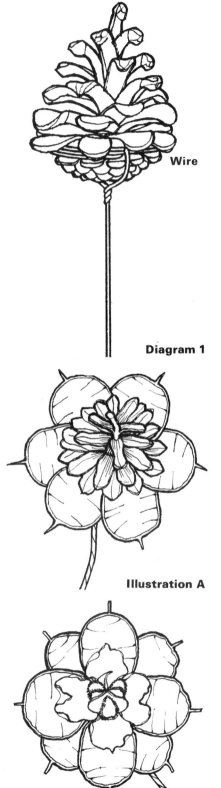

Wire

Diagram 1

Illustration A

Illustration B

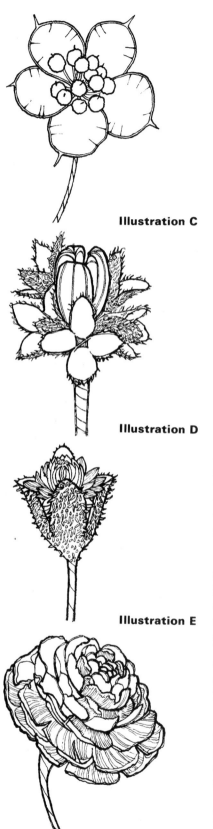

Illustration C

Illustration D

Illustration E

Illustration F

almost too pretty to ignore. The one we show in illustration F looks just like a perfect, pale brown rose. It has a tight bud-like centre, beautifully shaped 'petals', and slightly curled edges. And another thing — it will look like that for ever. We couldn't resist it. We cut a slice off the base to 'flatten' the shape, then simply wired it and bound the stem.

Preserved leaves, turning the rich deep colours of autumn can be used as petals to make most attractive 'flowers'. Illustration G, page 52 shows glycerined mahonia leaves, but you could copy the idea with leaves from your garden or ones you can find on a country walk. Beech leaves, of course, are among the most popular for preserving, and could be used perfectly well in this way.

To preserve the leaves, it is essential to cut them in July or early August. First split the stems, then stand them overnight in warm water. Mix one part glycerine to two parts very hot water. Stand the sprays — about four branches — in this substance, in an earthenware crock or jam jar for about two weeks. You will be able to see when the leaves start becoming tacky and take on a wax-like appearance. Remove them from the container, wash and dry the stems and leave them to dry — about two to three weeks. You can then use them either as described here, leaf by leaf, or in arrangements with other dried flowers.

The mahonia leaves surround a 'Shoo-Fly' seed pod. This is wired first. Then each leaf is wired separately. To do this, push a fine wire through the leaf from the back, loop it in the front of the leaf over the central vein and out again at the back of the leaf. You will have to do this with great care to avoid splitting the leaf. Twist the short end of the wire tightly around the longer end. Arrange six or seven wired leaves round the wired seed pod, adjusting them until you are satisfied with the effect, then twist all the wires together to form a tight, neat stem. Bind this in the usual way.

The last of our 'nearly-natural' flowers is on a much bigger scale than the others, and is invaluable for large arrangements such as pedestals when fresh flowers are in short supply or expensive (illustration H). It is made up of six skeletonised magnolia leaves (which you can buy in many floral art shops and through flower clubs) surrounding a dried thistle pod. The thistle is firmly wired first, and then the flimsy, papery leaves are glued at the base and stuck all round it, slightly overlapping each other. Again the stem is bound with brown crêpe or floral tape.

To show you one way to use a selection of these flowers made from natural materials, we built up the candle arrangement you can see on page 52. This is made on a half-cylindrical strip of foam (Styrofoam) and would make a delightful table centrepiece for autumn or Christmas time.

First of all, position the candle roughly one-third of the distance from one end of the block. To secure it, scoop out a hole with a nail file, and then partially fill it with Plasticine pushed in firmly to make a shallow well. Press the candle into

Tiny 'primroses' on a boater, cut from starched Liberty lawn

Illustration G

Illustration H

this, and build up more Plasticine around it to form a 'collar'.

Next, decide on the position of the apples; two close to the candle and one further along. You could, of course, wire the apples and stick the wire into the foam base, but that phrase about 'waste not, want not' must have prevented us from doing so. We took the slightly more laborious course, and built up little mounds of Plasticine, like miniature egg cups, to hold the apples firmly in place. Then they are still fit to eat!

The apples seemed to suggest a circular theme to the whole arrangement, especially after we had surrounded each one with mini cones. Choose ones with short stalks attached, and simply push them into the Plasticine. If your cones do not have stalks, wire them as described.

Next, we positioned a well-formed fir cone almost at the right-hand edge of the block, and surrounded it with a ring of grass seed heads. Just as the dark fir cones contrast well with the pale green apples, so the pale creamy grasses look well against the cone.

Bunch up ten or twelve heads of hare's tail grass, twist a wire round the stems and stick them under the candle; do the same thing again; stick the wire into the foam block, on the right; follow the photograph for positioning.

Fill in the arrangement with 'nearly-natural' flowers. We used one with the seed-pod centre and another with the bluey-black cluster of ivy seed pods.

With all these circular 'motifs', we decided it was time for a change. See how important the spiky mahonia-leaf flower has become, nestling against the white candle.

Use more cones — all on their own stalks — clusters of white dried statice, and frondy, feathery grasses to fill up all the spaces until the original foam block is completely covered. Lastly, position the skeletonised magnolia leaves to soften the outlines.

7 Flower Pictures

Flowers have always been a favourite subject for pictures in all forms of art, ranging from paintings by Old Masters to present-day fabric collages. And so no book about flowers would be complete without a chapter about flower pictures.

But ours are no ordinary pictures. The first one is made of shells — lovely mauvy-blue mussel shells and pale pinky-white cockle shells which, it may surprise you, have the most natural and pretty-looking petal shapes — if you have any artistic imagination! The next picture comes straight out of the storecupboard. This time the petals are formed of pasta, beans and peppercorns, stuck on a paper doily and mounted on card — a colourful design full of textural interest. Pressed flowers and dried flowers, perhaps more familiar subjects, form the basis of the other two picture groups, the dried flowers enhancing faded old family photographs and looking for all the world like Victorian Valentines.

With the scope extending here from macaroni to mussels it is easy to see that you can make flower pictures from practically anything. Look enquiringly at sea-polished pebbles you find on the beach. Some of the smooth, oval ones are shaped just like petals, and can be found in almost as many colours as flowers themselves; beads, used either geometrically or in clusters, can be mounted in flower patterns on card or fabric backgrounds, and even household string, tightly coiled or frayed into frondy shapes, can be made to look remarkably like dandelion clocks or cow parsley seed heads. Follow the designs on these pages and let them inspire you into a whole new realm of flower pictures.

SHELL PICTURE

We used a highly decorative old frame that had, artistically speaking, far outlived the picture it surrounded. This gave us the feeling for the shell picture, a soft curve of simple shapes (photograph A, page 54). But even without this adornment, the shells and the pattern they make are attractive enough to stand on their own in a very simple setting.

If you plan to dismantle and re-use an old picture frame, this is what to do. Remove the picture and the backing and make a new background. You can use a fabric, as we did — in this case, a deep pink poplin — or paper mounted on card; hardboard used on the 'wrong' — textured — side and painted with two coats of household emulsion paint; plywood sealed or painted; coloured cardboard, or even white card — though in this case you would have to choose the colour of your shells very carefully to ensure that they contrasted with it well enough. Before deciding, it is a good idea to sort through your collection

A

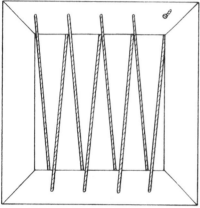

Diagram 1

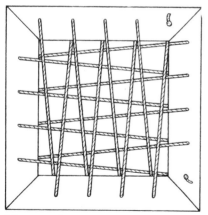

Diagram 2

of shells, pick out a few that you would like to use and try them against different coloured backgrounds. You will soon see whether an almost monochromatic colour scheme or a more striking contrast pleases you more.

The newly-covered backing can be put into position straight away, and you can work with the frame surrounding it – this might help you to visualise the finished effect – or you can mark out very carefully on the backing where the inner edge of the frame comes (do this about $\frac{1}{8}$-inch inside the lines, so that the pencil mark won't show) and complete your picture before framing it.

In any event, measure the card (it must be white if you are going to cover it with fabric), board or wood very carefully so that it fits accurately within the frame, and cut it out exactly. A craft knife, with removable blade, is the best tool for cutting card. If you are covering it with fabric, cut this oversize, leaving about $1-1\frac{1}{2}$ inches overlap round all the edges. Stretch the fabric over the base so that it is taut, and hold it in position with a few long tacking stitches, right across the back, both lengthwise and widthways. Using a strong thread, and pulling each stitch very tightly, sew across the back, both up and down, and from side to side, crisscrossing the stitches so that you finish with a trellis effect of vertical and horizontal threads (Diagrams 1 and 2). Remove the tacking stitches. This method is far more satisfactory than sticking the fabric, when air bubbles and creases are likely to spoil the smooth finish that is so essential.

If you want to cover the backing with paper, choose a strong quality. Thin papers will give disappointing results and may prove not strong enough to hold the weight of the shells and the adhesive. Using the glue sparingly, spread it evenly on both surfaces, that is on the backing and the paper, leave the surfaces to become tacky for about five or ten minutes and then put them together, smoothing them out carefully.

Selecting your shells

Although we used only about seventy-five shells for our picture, it is important to have far more to choose from. The success of your picture will depend upon your being able to grade the shells for size and colour, so that they go together as perfectly as the petals of a flower. If you are collecting your shells from beaches and riverbeds – and not buying them from a specialist shop – this is the way to treat them. All molluscs with living creatures inside must be boiled as soon as possible after collection. A few minutes is sufficient. The shellfish can be extracted with a small knife if they are bi-valves (molluscs with two shells, joined as if by a hinge: for example, clams, mussels, oysters, cockles, tellins, scallops, lucines and piddocks), or dug out with a bent pin if they fall into the other main shell group, the gastropods. This group is generally coiled, with a single shell, and includes whelks, snails, cowries, wentletraps, periwinkles, top-shells, conches, limpets and abalones.

Clean the shells in warm water, scrubbing lightly with a nail brush before sorting into the different categories. Store them in layers of tissue or crêpe paper in shallow containers, like shoe-box lids or chocolate boxes.

Stained glass window flowers. Inset *Hanging ball using dried flowers and grasses*

55

B

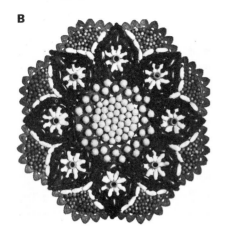

With the natural beauty of their colour, shape, texture, and markings, shells should never be painted. The subtle creams, greys, browns and yellows, the delicate pinks and oranges, the pearly whites and blues can never be bettered by colours from a paintbox — and scarcely by colours from a flower garden, either.

In our shell picture, we have used augers, mussels, tellins, cockles, winkles and cowries and small pieces of coral. If you do not have all of these in your collection it is not important. What matters is that you should have a pleasing balance. Note that the shells forming the wings of the butterfly and moth, the mussel shells making the three pairs of petals on the large flower, and even the tiny shells representing the leaves, all match for size and shape.

To achieve this, and to save time and temper when you are working out your design, grade each type of shell in your collection for colour; select the pinky, yellowy and white ones, for instance, and put them in separate piles — and then sub-grade these for size, small, medium and large.

For the shell picture you will need:
Background as described, it must be plain; a selection of shells; green garden wire to emulate stalks; adhesive; pair of tweezers

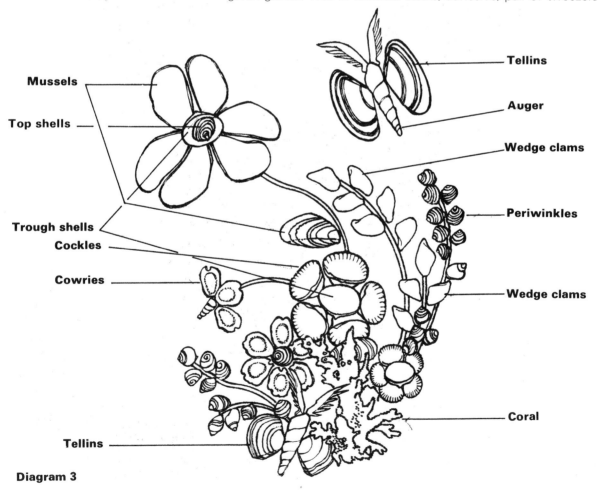

Diagram 3

to pick up small shells: brown gummed paper strip. Unless you are a natural artist, it is advisable to sketch out first the outline of your design. If your frame has an oval mount, as ours did, you will want your picture to follow those curves. Angular designs within this framework would look quite out of place.

Once you have roughed out your picture, start sorting the shells, matching pairs or groups and ruthlessly overlooking any that are damaged or simply do not 'go' with the others. To avoid confusion later on, correspondingly number the place on the design and the back of each shell in pencil. The key to our shell picture (Diagram 3) will help you to identify the types of shells we used.

When you are satisfied with your design, start transferring it on to the picture backing. Begin by placing the wires for the stalks. Using an orange stick or cocktail stick with a sharp point, spread the thinnest possible trail of glue along each length of wire. Be very careful when you do this, because any over-run will show up on the picture and look as if a snail has crawled across it.

Before gluing each shell, place it, either face down or lying on its back, as it will appear and then look at it carefully to see where it actually touches the background. Spread a very little glue only where it is needed, and be sure to put the shells down exactly where you want them to stay. Use a pair of tweezers to pick up the small shells.

Where groups of shells have others balancing on top of them, as in the case of the flowers, allow the underneath shell to dry before placing the upper ones, and again check to see just where the glue will be needed.

Leave the picture flat on a table for at least an hour after placing the last shells.

Cover the join between the frame and the backing, round all the four sides, with strips of brown gummed paper.

BEAN FLOWER PICTURE

We move from the beach to the kitchen for a colourful flower pattern made from a handful of dry stores. If you keep your beans, pasta and spices in glass jars on a shelf, you will probably already have realised how decorative they are, and what a wonderful range of colours they span. Indeed, they make an interesting and decorative focal feature in the room just as they are. If, however, you use your dry goods straight from the packet, you might be surprised to find how attractive they are. When you are adding two ounces of something to a mixing bowl in a hurry, it is not the best time to arouse your artistic flair.

If your own storecupboard does not offer up enough variety to make a 'bean' picture like ours (photograph B), a trip to the local supermarket or, better still, Indian grocer's, will soon bridge the gap. Even half a pound of beans, an ounce of some of the spices, will be more than enough, and give you some to spare for new recipes.

But before spending any money, look at what you have in stock. Lentils vary in colour from green-browns to the more familiar orange; split peas come in pale orange as well as in a

c

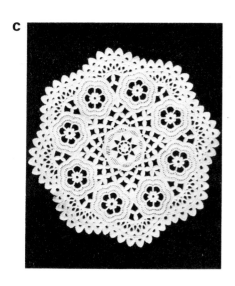

faded green; butter beans and dried haricot beans are soft, creamy-white; allspice are deep chestnut-brown; juniper berries, a glorious blueberry blue; peppercorns both black and nearly white; coriander and cardamom seeds a useful neutral colour, too. More colourful still, there are the red kidney beans (the kind you use for chilli con carne) and other beans, such as the black-eyed ones, which are to all intents and purposes 'patterned'. Notice how pretty cloves are. If you cut off the star-shaped tops and use them for decoration – and they look like little flowers themselves – you can use the remainder in cooking as usual. Then there are all the pastas. Not just the long, thin spaghetti strips, though this can be useful in geometrical patterns, but all the shapes, like shells, wheels, stars, letters of the alphabet, even, and, more simply as we show here, macaroni tubes.

Look in the garden shed for picture material, too. A few seeds left over in a packet from last year – with diminishing hopes of germinating, now – might be just what you want. Our picture shows the long, flat melon seeds (which we scooped out of a Honeydew melon and left to dry). You could use pumpkin seeds, too, a lovely corally colour, sunflower seeds or some of the larger vegetable seeds.

It is important to balance your picture with some richly coloured seeds or beans, some with an interesting texture, and some in neutral colours to allow the others to steal the limelight. We chose bright red beans for our strongest colour, dramatically surrounded by black peppercorns, and the rough, gravelly texture of yellow crystallised mimosa flowers for the 'surface interest'. Coriander seeds (or you could use white peppercorns which, being slightly larger, are easier to handle) provide the neutral tones.

Since most beans and seeds are relatively small, it could be confusing to try to 'paint' a freehand picture with them. To overcome this problem we started with an ordinary paper doily which already had a flower design and simply followed the outlines with the beans and seeds. The doily was white (see photograph C) but we coloured it with full-strength black Indian ink.

Another idea, which will certainly appeal to children – you could base your design on a geometric pattern of the kind drawn by the Spirograph pen-and-wheel equipment. Many of the shapes, incredibly intricate looking curves and arcs, actually look very much like multi-petalled flowers and would lend themselves, ideally in scale, to the use of small beans and seeds.

We stuck the doily on to thick card, leaving plenty of 'air' all around it, and then covered the doily, area by area with an adhesive, before pressing the beans into place.

If children are to work a bean picture, and they find this intricate method rather too tricky, you could give them a block of putty to work on. To do this, roll out the putty in an even thickness of no more than $\frac{1}{4}$-inch on a thick board and trim it neatly round the edges with a sharp knife. Scratch a design on the surface of the putty with a sharp-pointed nail or skewer, and then let the children proceed according to the directions given below.

Three portraits in designs using dried flowers

For a bean picture you will need :

Paper doily or other design to follow, as described; black Indian ink to colour doily if used; selection of beans and pasta, as described above; adhesive; white card for mounting; pair of tweezers for handling small seeds.

Paint the doily black with Indian ink and allow to dry. Stick to a piece of stiff white card, carefully cut to leave a good allowance all round the doily.

Work from the centre out towards the edges of the design, and take great care not to 'jog' the section you have just completed, and dislodge the seeds.

Cover small areas at a time with the adhesive and allow to become tacky (for about five minutes) before positioning the seeds.

If you are following our picture and Diagram 4, start in the centre with one single mimosa flower. Follow with a ring of six, then a ring of twelve, and lastly, eighteen. The next two 'open' rings of mimosa positioned themselves, one on each 'hole' in the doily pattern.

Next, outline the daisy shapes with the shiny red kidney beans. Make an eight-petalled flower in the centre of each one with melon seeds. Put a slice of macaroni ring and a black peppercorn in the centre of each flower, and a black peppercorn between each of the petals.

Outline the red beans with a line of black peppercorns,

Diagram 4

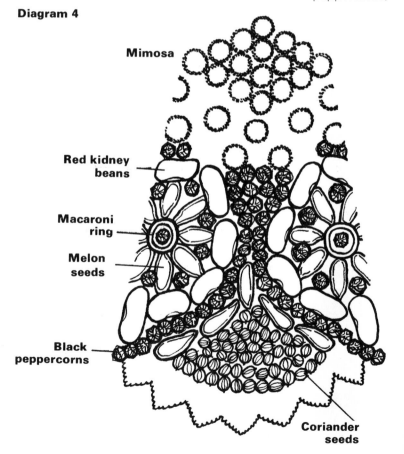

Mimosa

Red kidney beans

Macaroni ring

Melon seeds

Black peppercorns

Coriander seeds

coming to a point at the outside edge of the doily. Next position the rows of melon seeds, five or six making a curved V shape. Finally, fill in the outside 'triangles' with coriander seeds or white peppercorns.

Frame your bean picture in a simple box frame, the kind you can buy cheaply from chain stores, and hang it in the kitchen to remind you how beautiful are the materials at your fingertips!

FAMILY PORTRAITS

You can use pressed and dried flowers as part of a design incorporating portraits, photographs cut from magazines, or picture collages. The flowers create a third dimension and add a touch of romance.

We chose to show our three portraits on the shelves of an old pine cupboard — see the colour photograph facing page 58 surrounded by pretty glass and trinkets. They would look equally at home on one of those lovely old Victorian what-nots, on any small bookcase, or mounted together inside a large picture frame. In this case, cover the backing with a plain fabric, perhaps linen or velvet, in a colour to tone with the paper backgrounds of your portrait cards.

All our three portraits were unearthed from a box of family treasures where they had lain hidden for years. No such luck in your attic? Then you could set aside the ancestry factor and buy a few early postcard portraits from a junk shop. You can often find them in huge leather family photograph albums, going for a song.

Baby in a towel (photograph D)

Cut a piece of cartridge paper large enough to enclose the photograph and to be folded in half, like a greetings card. Cover one side of the card with brown wrapping paper. Score the inside of the card lightly with a craft knife before you fold it in half. Decide how large and what shape hole to cut out by positioning the photograph on the card, at equal distances from the top and bottom and from each side. Make a 'mask' by cutting a rough shape from an old postcard, until you are satisfied that the photograph will be shown to its best advantage. It is worth taking trouble to display a photograph taken in 1886!

Mark out the shape and cut through the brown paper and cartridge paper, using curved nail scissors for the curved edges and ordinary scissors for the straight lines.

Paste the photograph on the inside of the card, checking its position carefully before sticking it down. You might find you have to weight it down to make it stick.

Stick the photograph in position inside the card and slip a piece of paper in to protect it.

On a spare piece of paper, measure squares and then mark spots to indicate where the flowers are to go. Place this pattern over the front of the card and pierce through with a sharp pencil. Dab each mark with a tiny spot of glue, using an orange stick or cocktail stick, and position the glixia flowers and Briza Mini seed heads carefully. Do not try to slide the flowers across the paper once they have touched it; you will leave a glue smear. Leave the card flat on a table while the glue dries.

D

E

Dark-haired baby (photograph E, page 61)

We used a deep yellow card for this portrait of a baby, taken in about 1914. Fold the card in half, with the fold down the left-hand side. Using nail scissors, carefully cut round all the corners. To do this accurately, draw the shapes first with a coin.

Cut out a heart shape from paper. (The trick is to fold the paper in half lengthways and then cut through two layers. In this way, the heart will be symmetrical.) When you are satisfied with the shape and have checked that it adequately covers the baby's portrait, draw round it on the face of the yellow card.

Paste the photograph on the inside of the card so that it is perfectly framed by the heart shape. Slip a spare piece of paper inside the card to protect the photograph.

Surround the heart by dried or pressed flowers, using the most interesting one as a focal point at the bottom centre. It is important to keep the arrangement the same on both sides, so divide your flower material into pairs, matching leaves and sprays for size and shape. Stick the flowers, leaves and grasses in position with a very little adhesive, again applied with a cocktail or orange stick. Allow some of the flowers to overlap the heart shape, breaking up the outline.

F

Turn-of-the-century lady

This portrait of an elegant lady, *circa* 1902, is shown in appropriately sepia tones. The card mount is cut from dark yellow ochre paper, the kind used for office files, and the decoration is a ring of orangey-brown glixia and the cut-off heads of Briza Max, with Lagarus (hare's tails) at the top and Phalaris at the base. You can buy these dried grasses in florist's shops.

For variation, we decided to cut this card with a dome-shaped top. Position your photograph on a piece of card to estimate the size, fold the card in half and then draw a semi-circle shape at the top. You will find that a saucer or small tea plate is the right size for this. Cut through both thicknesses, just inside the pencil line so that it won't show. Draw a circle and cut it out of the front of the card.

Outline the circle with glixia flower heads and then with a ring of the large, fluffy heads of Briza Max alternated with single glixia heads. Stick a fan of five hare's tails grass heads at the top, with the largest one in the centre, the smallest ones at the outside. Complete the design with two heads of Phalaris stuck on at the base.

When sticking on the flowers and grasses, be sure not to let any glue stray on to the card where it will show.

If you want to mount all the 'framed' photographs in one frame, stick the two layers of card together before arranging and sticking the flowers.

PRESSED FLOWER PICTURE

If you press flowers from your garden or the hedgerows, you can create an artificial flower of a kind — a single-plane rather than a three-dimensional flower, that is. You can pick flowers for pressing all the year round but, since it is important to choose

Attractive wreath using bright paper flowers, fir cones and dried grasses

a dry day, and not to gather the flowers while the dew is still on them, winter conditions are rarely ideal. Pick flowers after noon, when they will be fully open, remembering that some flowers, like marigolds, close up towards evening. You will want to catch them before then.

Take a jar or bucket of water with you, so that you can keep the flowers fresh as you gather them. You want to dry them under carefully controlled conditions, not to let them wither before your eyes, so treat them as soon after picking as possible.

Snip off the stalks of each bloom before pressing. Or, in the case of long spiky formations, such as delphinium and larkspur, snip off each floret and treat it as a separate flower. Only those flowers with hard, thick middles resist pressing, as it is not possible to enclose the petals tightly between the sheets of absorbent paper. To dry these flowers you will have to pick off each petal separately and press them, without overlapping. Snip each leaf from its stem.

Blotting paper is the best material to use for pressing flowers, although children often settle for newsprint. Buy the blotting paper in large quantities — by the quire — and you will not find it expensive.

Do not try to crowd too many flowers or leaves on to each sheet of blotting paper. If you are pressing a quantity of flowers of a similar type, keep these together and label them on the outside. It is surprising how difficult it is to recognise them when you remove them weeks later. You might need to use two layers of blotting paper top and bottom when dealing with extra-fleshy flowers and leaves.

When you have arranged the flowers, petals and leaves carefully between the sheets of blotting paper, press each one between the pages of a heavy book, or put them on a flat surface and weight them — not too heavily — with an iron, bricks or a large stone. You will want to exert even pressure over the whole area — this is why books are really best.

Leave the flowers undisturbed — no peeping — in a light, airy room. Avoid at all costs putting them in a damp place. Small, delicate flowers will be dried within about four weeks but the larger ones will take at least six weeks. You must curb your impatience and leave them undisturbed all this while.

You will need some stalks for your pressed flower picture. Dry the supple stalks of clover, daisy, buttercup, primrose and clematis *montana* specially for this purpose.

For the pressed flower picture you will need:
White or coloured card for mounting the flowers etc.; pressed and dried flowers, leaves and stalks as available; clear adhesive; picture frame and glass.

You will have to design your picture according to the dried materials you have available. Try to balance the colours and textures and try, above all, not to crowd the flowers too closely together. There is all the difference between a picture that looks as if the flowers and leaves have been lightly scattered about by a gentle breeze and one which looks as if they have been tipped in a heap from a sack!

As you can see from photograph G, our picture radiates from a central arrangement of overlapping leaves, with a single clematis flower on top of them. When you are superimposing flowers or grasses on top of leaves, choose ones which contrast well in colour so that you will clearly be able to see the outline of both.

Unless you are aiming at a definitely assymetrical arrangement, such as an L shape, balance the weight and the colours of the material on both sides. You will find that flowers spanning all the seasons blend quite happily in a picture — here you see buttercups, daisies, pansies, vetch, honeysuckle and a variety of leaves and grasses.

It is a good idea to try out the arrangement on a piece of white paper first, before sticking the material in place. Then you can adjust and re-adjust the individual pieces until you have a flower 'painting' that pleases you.

Put a tiny dab of clear adhesive — again using a matchstick — along the length of the stems or in the centre of a flower and at the tops of the petals. Use the glue very sparingly indeed. Frame the picture in the usual way.

8 It's the Shape That Counts

Although flower and leaf decorations in spheres, rings and circles are part of our tradition, they have never been easier to make than they are now. We can re-create the idea of a holly wreath to hang on the front door without having to make a wire and moss frame for it; our design of dried fir cones, black-wisp corn and paper flowers (see the colour photograph facing page 62) is built on a foam ring.

The very name pomander conjures up a picture of a pretty decoration wafting sweet, pungent smells. Somehow, there is something intensely feminine about them, like pot pourri, no longer a necessity but a little luxury to have around the house. We copied the feel (though not, unfortunately, the aroma) of a pomander in the hanging ball decoration (also shown in colour opposite page 54), using tiny paper flowers, dried grasses, dried flowers, cobnuts and ribbon. This decoration, too, owes its simplicity to a foam block, a complete sphere ready and waiting for any number of adaptations.

The third arrangement in this chapter uses a foam cone. As the design took shape, it reminded us of a metronome, and so we photographed it, just for fun, on sheet music. The flowers are easy to 'mass produce' and cut out several at a time. This is essential. However keen one is, enthusiasm for any pattern tends to abate when cutting the two hundredth petal! There is no such danger here. As you can see, all the flowers suggested throughout the chapter are simple all-in-one designs. It's the way they are used . . . it's the shape that counts.

FLOWER WREATH
Happy Christmas with a welcoming wreath on the front door. Choose the colour of the tissue paper flowers to match the colour of the door — not forgetting your hall colour scheme too.

For the flowers you will need:
Tissue paper in various colours (ours were deep blue, turquoise, mauve, yellow and white); tracing paper or greaseproof paper; pencil; card for template; scissors; transparent self-adhesive tape; glass-headed pins.

Trace the patterns given for the three different types of flower (Diagrams 1–3). Cut card templates for the circles, trace in the petal details, and cut out of the templates the petal shapes for one quarter section of each flower, as indicated.

Pattern 1, the flower with the most pointed petals, is cut from four layers of tissue paper. Place them all on top of each other, and cut out a circle. Fold the circle in half and then into quarters, use the template again to draw round the petal shapes, and cut these out through all the layers. Unfold once, back into semi-circles, bring the two sides together and secure on the outside with a tiny ($\frac{1}{4}$-inch) strip of sticky tape to form a cone. Push a finger into the centre of the cone to open out the shape, and pierce with a glass-headed pin. Make about twelve of these flowers to use on the wreath.

Pattern 2 makes a flower the same size, but it has fewer, flatter petals. It is cut from only two layers of tissue paper — we used white and yellow. Make the flower exactly as described for Pattern 1, fasten into a cone shape and pierce with a glass-headed pin. Make about fourteen flowers for the wreath.

Pattern 3 is the largest flower in this group, based on a 3-inch diameter circle. Use four layers of tissue paper for this flower — ours were dark blue, turquoise, mauve and white in different combinations. Notice that for this flower, to make the petals more 'frilly' than the others, you have to make deeper cuts, closer together.

For the leaves you will need:

Scraps of dark green felt (or brown if you prefer); picture wire or fine wire; fabric adhesive; tracing paper or greaseproof paper; pencil; thin card for template; scissors.

Trace the leaf pattern (Diagram 4), transfer the outline on to the card and cut out the template. From the green felt, cut two shapes for each leaf. You will need between 25 and 30 leaves for the wreath.

Cut a 3-inch piece of wire for each leaf and straighten out each length. Position a piece of wire down the centre of a leaf shape (see Diagram 5) and, using fabric adhesive, place another leaf shape on top, making sure you get the two pieces directly on top of each other. Place the completed leaves under heavy weights until the glue is dry. Holding the top and bottom of each leaf between the thumb and first finger of each hand, slightly bend the wire to make the leaf curl in a natural shape.

For the wreath you will need:

A ring of foam (Styrofoam), approximately 10-inch diameter;

Diagram 5

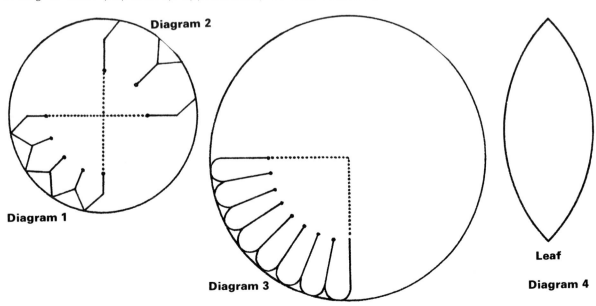

Diagram 2

Diagram 1

Diagram 3

Leaf

Diagram 4

Diagram 6

Bend
wires
under

extra, small block of the foam; green poster paint; stiff paint brush; tissue paper flowers and felt leaves, as above; selection of fir cones; grass and wheat heads (we used Briza Max, Phalarus and black-wisp corn); wire for cones and to hang wreath on door.

Rub the foam ring with the spare piece of foam to smooth away any sharp edges. Continue until all the edges are neatly rounded. Leave the back of the block flat, as it is. This makes for easier assembly and hanging. Paint the foam ring with two coats of the green poster paint, pushing it well into the surface. You will need to apply the paint liberally as the foam absorbs it quickly.

Unless the cones are complete with little 'branches', wire each one, twisting the wire in the middle of its length, twice round the inside of the first row of 'petals' (Diagram 6). Start by positioning the cones in the block, using the largest ones in the central positions and matching each pair on either side accurately for size and shape. For instance, it would quite spoil your arrangement if you had large and small cones, or closed and fully-opened ones used at random. Push the cones into the block so that they rest close up to the surface.

To secure each cone, either wrap the wires round the foam ring and twist the ends together at the back, or push the two wires through, a little distance apart and tie together at the back. Otherwise the weight of the cone will pull out the wire. If you like, you can make a small hollow bed of Plasticine for them to rest on. Just push the Plasticine firmly against the foam.

Next arrange the 'fan' shape of the wheat ears, cutting the lengths of the stalks so that you have the greatest height in the centre and short pieces towards the sides. Follow the photograph closely for the positioning.

Fill in the shape between the cones with the paper flowers, each one pierced with a glass-headed pin. Arrange the flowers in clusters, matching each side as you did with the cones.

Complete the outline by arranging the leaves and pushing them in so that they completely cover the edges of the foam block, both inside and outside the ring. Adjust and re-adjust the flowers and leaves until this is achieved.

To hang the wreath on a wall, push two doubled-up wires through the foam block at equal distances from the centre top. Twist the wire to form fairly tight loops so that they can be hung at the back on picture hooks. It is obviously advisable to do this before you start the arrangement.

One wire pushed through the top and twisted into a loop will be enough if you want to hang the wreath on a door. You can conceal and decorate the wire with ribbon and suspend it from the door knocker.

HANGING BALL

Another design combining paper flowers and natural materials, this is our version of a pomander – even the glixia flowers are the colour of a shrivelled orange! This decoration looks charming hanging from some shiny Christmas ribbon. Place the hanging ball in the centre of an archway, between bookshelves or low over a dining table where there is no ceiling-hung light fitting for an effective decoration.

For the flowers you will need:

Pale yellow tissue paper or toilet roll tissue; tracing paper or greaseproof paper; pencil; thin card for template; scissors.

You might decide that you need not make a template for this simple little primrose shape (Diagram 7). If so, you can trace the outline, reverse the tracing on to your paper and go over the lines with a pencil. You will find the curved blades of nail scissors particularly suitable.

You can 'mass produce' this flower by folding over the paper until you have, say, six thicknesses, and then cutting through all the layers at once. In the case of toilet paper, you can cut twelve flowers at a time. You will need approximately forty flowers for the decoration.

For the hanging ball you will need:

A ball of foam (Styrofoam) approximately 5 inches in diameter; paper flowers, as above; dried flowers such as orange glixia, white heather-type statice and achillea; cobnuts; hare's tail grass (*Lagarus*); green ribbon (we used shiny Christmas ribbon); fine wire; knitting needle; darning needle; Plasticine.

The easiest way to decorate the foam ball is to have it suspended in front of you so that you can turn it round as you work. You *can* hang it from the ceiling, but then it will swing away from you and resist any attempt to push awkward stalks into it.

We found that the best way was to slice a small piece from the bottom, mark the top centre with a pencil and drive a medium knitting needle through from top to bottom. Cut a length of doubled fine wire, at least 2 inches longer than the diameter of the ball. Take out the knitting needle through the hole; push the wire with the looped end at the base. Spread loop out over the hole to stop wire falling off. Then push knitting needle back. Leave at least 4 inches sticking out from the base of the ball and embed this in a mound of Plasticine or putty. Stick the Plasticine on to an old plate, and then you can move the ball round as you need to (Diagram 8).

Draw a pencil line round the ball, dividing it in half, and then divide each section into three, drawing pencil lines right round. This will give you the position of the ribbon strips and the six segments which are decorated alternately with paper flowers and natural materials.

Begin by positioning the cobnuts. You will need about eight or ten for each of the three sections. If you cannot obtain these nuts, you can equally well use acorns, beech masts or tiny fir cones — any of the small brown fruits of autumn, in other words. Pierce a hole in the ball with a darning needle where you want to stick each nut. Choose cones, beech masts or nuts that still have small stalks which you can use. Cut them off to a length of no more than $\frac{5}{8}$-inch. Any longer than this, and they will snap off as soon as you apply any pressure.

We bought a pound of cobnuts from the greengrocers, selected the ones with stalks, and put the others to delicious culinary use.

Fill in the gaps between the nuts with the fluffy, rounded heads of hare's tail grass. Again, cut off the stalks to just over $\frac{1}{2}$-inch and pierce a hole with a darning needle before pushing

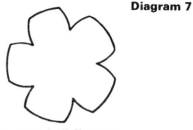

Diagram 7

Hanging ball flower

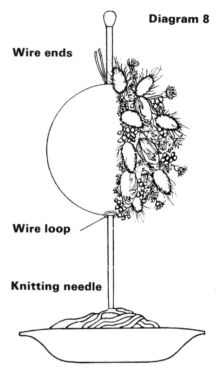

Diagram 8

Wire ends

Wire loop

Knitting needle

Metronome flower

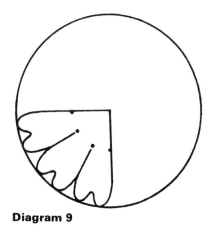

Diagram 9

them in. Push the stalks in at the angle you want them to be — remember that they are not flexible and will not twist or bend.

Cut the white statice and achillea into tiny sprigs and the glixia stalks varying from just over 1-inch to about $\frac{3}{8}$-inch long. Fill in the gaps with clusters of these dried flowers, making sure that the surface is completely covered. Follow the photograph closely — you will see that some of the glixia is pushed in close against the foam, and other flowers, on longer stalks, are used to break up the outline.

Now begin working on the other three segments. Cut the stalks of the glixia flowers, one for each paper flower, to $\frac{3}{8}$-inch long. Taking each paper flower separately, hold it in position against the foam ball, pierce a hole through the centre with a darning needle, and stick a glixia flower through to 'pin' it in place. Continue adding paper flowers and glixia so that the petals of the paper flowers overlap and completely conceal the foam.

Slot the ribbon through the lengths of wire and twist them to hold it in place. Wind the ribbon three times right round the ball, covering the pencil lines and working it gently between the decorations. Glue the two ends of wire together for about 5 or 6 inches at the top, to strengthen it, and finish off with a bow.

FLOWER CONE

We made our decoration a bold and positive colour statement in red, white, green and black. The cone is not literally a cone — though they are available — but a foam pyramid block. This gave us three flat surfaces to fill in with the red, white and green flowers, which we separated with single-flower strips of black.

The paper flowers are made on the now-familiar cone principle, a simple tissue paper circle, folded into a semi-circle and stuck to make a double cone. You could make them in other kinds of paper — crêpe, toilet paper or face tissues, or in starched cotton. They look lovely made from crisp organdie. (In this case, either buy a white foam cone or, if you cannot obtain one, paint a green one white. Otherwise the colour would show through the fabric.) Glass-headed pins are used again to position the flowers and they show, so make sure to use all the same colour for each section.

For the flowers you will need:

Tissue paper in four colours (red, white, green and black) or other paper or material of your choice; tracing or greaseproof paper; pencil; card for template; nail scissors and ordinary scissors; darning needle; transparent self-adhesive tape; glass-headed pins.

Trace the outline for the flower from Diagram 9, not forgetting to mark in the dots. Transfer the outline on to the card and pierce the dots with a darning needle to make a hole. Fold the paper until you have, say, eight thicknesses. Draw round the template and pierce through the holes with a sharp pencil point. Using the curved nail scissors, cut the flower shape through all the layers of paper. Then with the ordinary scissors, cut in from the petal edges to each dot. You will find that you have two 'scallops' in each petal section. Separate the eight layers so that you have eight flowers.

Fold each little circular flower shape in half, to make a semi-circle, and wrap it round to form a cone. Without overlapping the edges at all, secure with a $\frac{1}{4}$-inch strip of narrow sticky tape, as for the flowers for the wreath. Push your finger into the flower to make it into a full cone shape and pierce each one through the centre with a glass-headed pin.

Arrange the flowers on the cone in orderly rows, working on one section and with flowers of one colour at a time and pushing the points firmly in. When you have completed two-thirds of the cone, and to avoid squashing the flowers you have already positioned, stick something like an orange stick into the top of the cone so that you can hold it firmly while you press the remaining flowers in. Finish with a black flower on the top.

You could cover a rounded foam cone block with flowers in the same way, perhaps working them in a 'spiral staircase' arrangement, with the different colours cascading round and round the shape instead of in flat panels.

When working with foam blocks of this kind, it is as well to know that they do not take at all kindly to the use of strong adhesives. Many of the well-known brands on the market cause the foam to disintegrate completely, some immediately and some, mysteriously, overnight so that the next morning when you go to admire your handiwork, you find, instead, an object that looks as if the mice have tasted it.

Natural grasses are delightful in decorative shapes of the type described here. For information and inspiration, here is a pot pourri of some of the varieties to look for.

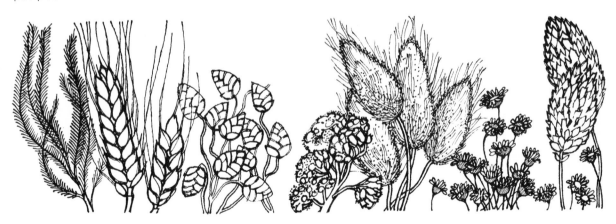

Stipa grass   **Wheat**   **Briza max**   **Achillea**   **Hare's tail grass**   **Glixia**   **Phalarus**

9 The Perfect Finish

As in all creative work, it is the preparation and the 'finish' you give to artificial flowers that will distinguish them from the ordinary. It is, someone's grandmother once said, just as quick to do a job properly as to do it badly. And so it is in flower making. Once you have read the general guideline in this chapter, and the specific directions for the pattern you are following, you will find it just as simple, and a great deal more rewarding to cut the patterns accurately, fix the centres securely and neatly to the wires, and bind the stems as unobtrusively as possible. Ragged petals, lumpy calyxes and uneven binding will never give you the feeling of satisfaction you deserve when you have spent precious time at your hobby.

Enough lecturing! Here are the few simple rules, and some general hints, to help you.

EQUIPMENT

A list of what you need precedes the instructions for each flower design. Some flowers will require a few items not listed below, but you will find that they are almost all of general household use, and you will not find yourself stuck for the very thing you need on a Sunday afternoon when all the shops are closed. The basic equipment can be summarised as this:

Wire: 7-inch rose wires, which you can buy in bundles from florist's shops; thicker, garden wire. More detail about wires later.

Scissors: Very sharp scissors are essential for accurate cutting, especially when you have to cut through several thicknesses of paper. Medium-sized ones are most useful. If children are helping with the flowers, reserve the use of sharp scissors to yourself. Pinking shears (serrated scissors) are useful but not essential for some of the patterns. Nail scissors, with curved blades, are the easiest to use for curved petal patterns and any 'rounded corners' you are required to cut. Again, ordinary scissors can be used.

Wire cutters: If you have some in the tool shed for garden use, now is the time to bring them indoors. There is quite a bit of wire cutting to do throughout the designs, and if you do not have any cutters it might be worth investing in a pair. Otherwise, if you use your household scissors, you will very soon have to replace those, anyway.

Pencils: Where there is a particular advantage in using a very soft, or a very hard pencil, this is specifically mentioned. Otherwise, make sure that you have a supply of pencils with very sharp points. That is the way to obtain a crisp, accurate outline.

Tracing paper: In nearly every chapter, you will find that you have to trace the flower pattern from the book and transfer it on to card to make a master pattern, or template (which is described below). Greaseproof paper is perfectly satisfactory for this, and a good deal cheaper than tracing paper which you can buy in artists' materials shops.

Card: Use old postcards or the plain backs of used cereal packets for the templates. Anything will do as long as it is stiff enough to hold the shape without curling or bending. Thicker card is recommended for picture mounting.

Glue: The main thing about the glue you use is that you use it very sparingly – more about that later. We found rubber adhesive satisfactory for most of the light-pressure work and heavy-duty contact adhesive where more strain was involved.

Waxing equipment: Full details of this process are given in Chapter 3. But basically all you need are an old saucepan and a supply of white household candles. A sugar boiling thermometer is useful, too, so that you can always be sure that the wax has reached just the right heat before you immerse the flowers and leaves.

Starch: We experimented with both spray starch, in aerosol cans, and powdered starch for the flowers in Chapter 4. Full details of the method, and the 'recipe' for powdered starch, are given there.

Accessories: Paper clips are useful to hold several layers of paper firmly together while you are cutting. A hair-curling pin is the best tool we found for curling the crêpe rose petals. You will need used matchsticks, orange sticks or cocktail sticks for applying glue, and the last two as alternatives for curling petals.

Paper and fabrics suitable for flower making: These are discussed in full below and in each chapter.

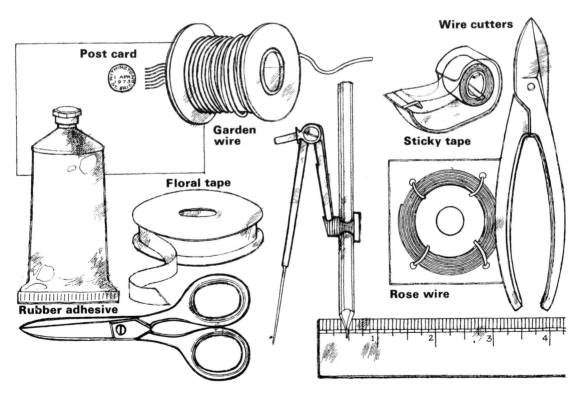

Post card

Garden wire

Floral tape

Rubber adhesive

Wire cutters

Sticky tape

Rose wire

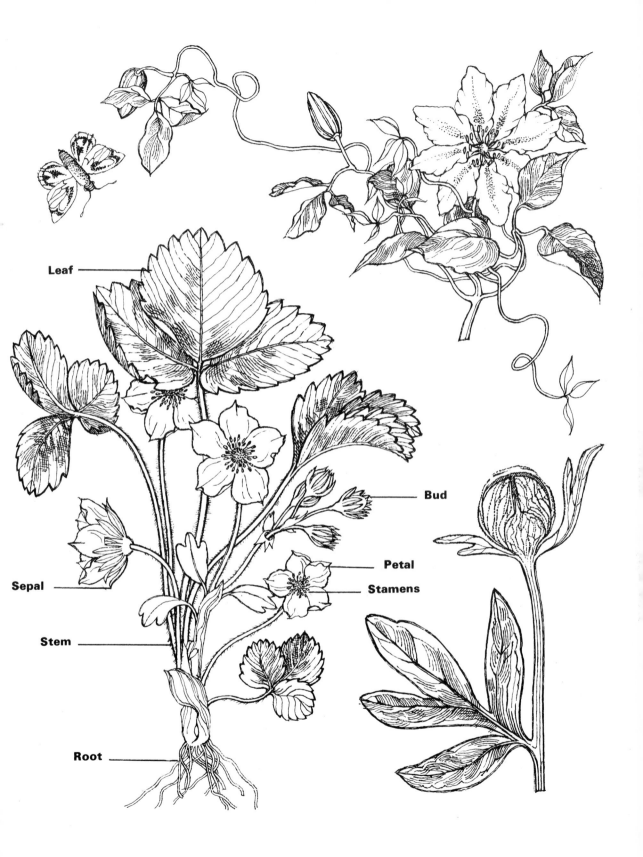

Leaf

Bud

Sepal

Petal

Stamens

Stem

Root

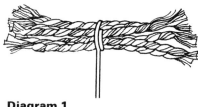

Diagram 1

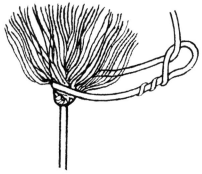

Diagram 2

Diagram 3

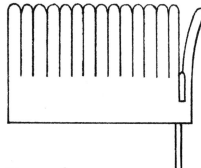

Diagram 4

Wiring

In every case, the wire used at the commencement of the flower design is the one you end with. A continuous wire is used for centres, petals and everything, and there is no need to change. Sometimes, though, an extra wire is needed to bind in sepals etc. The 7-inch fine rose wires are useful for tying and for small flower stems. Taping strengthens the stems, of course. Remember that once the rose wires are wrapped round flower centres and twisted, there will be a length of only about 5 inches for the stem. Soft, fine garden wire can be used. It is flexible and, being bought in a roll, can be cut to any length. It is strong enough for short stems, but not recommended for lengths of more than 4–5 inches. Fuse wire can be used in some cases if no other is available, but it is expensive to use in this way. Only the 5- and 10-amp thicknesses are flexible enough. PVC-covered garden wire is strong and pliable, and good for longer stems and has been used extensively for many designs. It can be bound just as the other wires are. Picture wire, 20-gauge (Welpak) is used for ivy leaf stems and for veins in leaves. One of the most important steps in all flower making is to make sure that the centre stays securely on the stem, and so neat wiring at this point is vitally important.

To hook a bundle of string, wool, raffia and so on to form a flower centre, always loop the wire *over* first, then hook the end up and cut (see Diagram 1). These directions apply throughout the book, wherever the instructions tell you to wire the string and raffia centres. You will find this method much more satisfactory than several untidy twists of wire.

To begin wiring a petal or stamen to the central stem, follow Diagram 2. First of all, make a loop in the end of the wire and twist the end firmly round. Pass the end of the wire through the loop. Pull it backwards to tighten it, and it will stay put. If you just wrap the wire round it will work its way loose. To join two short lengths of wire together, make a loop in the end of one, and twist the short end neatly to secure. Pass the end of the second wire through the loop and twist that short end round the long end to form a second loop (see Diagram 3). When wiring a fringed paper or fabric centre (that is for patterns where no beads or other such centres are included) hook the wire over the first cut in the paper, as shown in Diagram 4 and press to close up the hook tightly.

Glue and adhesive tape

Since many of the papers and the starched fabrics you will be using to make the flowers are flimsy and transparent, it is vital that you keep the glue only to the areas where it is needed. Always test first just where a flower will rest or how a pattern fits so that you know exactly where to glue. Except when you have to cover large, flat areas – such as covering cartridge paper and paper surfaces for the 'Valentine' cards – it is usually advisable to dab spots of glue on with a spent matchstick, or with an orange stick or cocktail stick. This way you have complete control on the amount of adhesive you use. It is much easier to put two or three small dabs if one is not enough than it is to remove unwanted smears and traces.

Far better results are obtained if you apply the glue to the surfaces and then leave it to become tacky — that is, at the stage when it is just beginning to set. The time needed for this will vary with the type of glue, from about five to twenty minutes. The rubber solution needs to be left for about five minutes and the stronger, contact adhesive up to ten minutes. Always make sure that you use a clear adhesive. The thick, white glues are not suitable for this type of work.

If you do find that you have areas of excess rubber solution, you can remove them carefully by rubbing with a small ball of the dried-up glue. It is worth accumulating the glue as it dries round the rim of the tin, for this purpose.

Where two edges have to be joined without overlapping (as is the case with tissue paper cone-pattern flowers) we recommend using self-adhesive transparent tape. Always use the minimum that will give you satisfactory results and, if your roll of tape happens to be wider than you need, cut strips in half lengthways. It is a good idea, when you are making a number of flowers together, to cut strips the right length and stick them to the back of your hand. Then you will be able to peel them off one by one as you need them, and will be in no danger of forgetting where you put them!

Sticking plaster has its uses in flower making, too. It gives a firm, non-slippery base for some of the larger flowers to grip on. You will find it recommended for taping bamboo canes before the tissue paper decorations are wired on.

If you have to use ordinary adhesive tape on the outside of a flower (though we have tried to avoid this) remember that, because it is shinier than the paper you will be using, it is not invisible. If necessary, it is best to use a double-sided sticky tape, and cover the top side with a strip of the same paper being used to make the flower, or try to buy the adhesive tape that is virtually invisible.

Paper and fabrics for flower making

Because you will want to experiment with designs of your own, and will possibly want to interchange some of the designs in the book, making them up in different materials from those suggested, it is as well to have an understanding of the properties of the papers and fabrics you will be working with.

Without doubt, crêpe paper is the most adaptable of the materials. It can be substituted for tissue paper, for the designs in Chapter 1, for the starched fabric flowers in Chapter 4, and for the tissue cone flowers in Chapter 8. But this is not a two-way traffic, and neither tissue paper nor cotton can be substituted for all the crêpe paper designs.

Only crêpe paper has the necessary qualities of being able to be curled, bent, stretched and frilled in just that way.

Crêpe paper: There are two grades. We recommend the 100 per cent stretch quality for the petals and the 60 per cent stretch for the leaves. As stated in the appropriate chapter, it pays to buy the best quality. Look carefully at the crêpe paper colours before you buy. Some of them are rather intense and you might not consider them appropriate for the more delicate flower designs. If you are considering Christmas or other decorations, you can buy silver and gold colours in crêpe. These could make quite interesting flowers.

Tissue paper: This is the paper to use for all kinds of colour effects. The range of forty colours gives you scope for subtle combinations of the same colour, or for startling and bold contrasts. The paper can successfully be bent to make large petal shapes — it is stiff enough to hold a large curve — and fringed to make fluffy centres. But it will not stretch and does tear more easily than crêpe. Any lightweight paper can be waxed and you could, if you wanted to, experiment with waxing small tissue paper flowers. Obviously, it would take a huge saucepan and a very large amount of candle wax to treat the decorations in the first chapter.

Transparent paper: The 'stained glass window' flowers have been designed to show off the beautiful effects made by light passing through different colour combinations of Cellophane paper. It is interesting to note that these effects are not always what you would expect to achieve, and the same mixture of paintbox colours does not produce the same result as combining those colours in this paper. This is why, in Chapter 5, we recommend you to hold layers of the different colours up to the light to see what colour you are producing.

Glistening paper: The 'leaded light' shapes for the stained glass window flowers can be cut from this type of paper, foil covered on one side and white on the other. It is available in gold, silver and other colours such as red and green. (But these colours would compete too much with the colour effects of the Cellophane.) You can also use gold or silver heavy-duty foil (Polyflex), which is coloured on both sides. It is sold in rolls, 21 inches wide and is strong and flexible, but not stiff. It is difficult for amateurs to handle if intricate patterns are being worked.

Matt papers: For the 'stained glass window' outlines you could use flint papers or enamel papers in dark colours, or any black, dark brown or other dark-coloured paper with a matt surface. Choose one that does not tear easily, as some of the 'lead strips' are rather narrow. It is also important that the paper will not allow any light to pass through.

Cotton fabrics: You can use organdie, lawn, sea island cotton, gingham or any other cotton fabric with a close-weave for the simple cone designs in Chapter 8. They would give a more 'drawing-room' quality to the cone and the hanging ball. All cottons need starching twice (following the directions given in full in Chapter 4) except organdie, which needs only one application. It is important to starch the fabric before cutting out the flower and other shapes, to cut down fraying to a minimum.

Making and using a template

To transfer the petal, sepal and leaf patterns from the book to your paper or fabric, you will need, in almost every case, to make a template. The best way to do it is to trace the outlines on to greaseproof or tracing paper, reverse the tracing on to a piece of plain card, and then cut out the shape. Use this template to cut out each pattern piece and you will be sure of complete uniformity.

Place your paper or fabric on a completely flat surface. Hold the template down with one hand and draw round it with a very sharp pencil point (photograph A). When marking on fabric, you can fix the template down with a small strip of double-sided sticky tape, peeling it off and moving it along the material to draw out more patterns.

Placing the template: To make the most of the stretch properties of crêpe paper, it is important to place the template correctly every time you cut out a pattern shape. As already pointed out in Chapter 2, crêpe paper has a right and a wrong side. The matt surface is the right side. Place the paper with this side downwards, and draw round the template on the wrong, shiny side. This avoids pencil outlines showing on the right side.

Crêpe paper can only be stretched or frilled across the grain, or diagonally. It is essential, therefore, to place the template with the top and bottom on the up-and-down way of the paper. Diagram 5 shows you the right and wrong way, and Diagram 6(a–d), the stretching, curling, compressing and frilling possible with this material.

Follow the same instructions when you are cutting petals from starched cotton, too. Keep the template straight along the fabric as you cut out each one, so that the grain is always running the same way. Do not cut fabric petals 'on the bias'.

Binding

The way you bind the flower stems is perhaps the most important single operation in flower making. Throughout the designs in the book we have suggested only two basic materials for this — narrow, $\frac{1}{4}$-inch strips of crêpe paper and floral tape. It is possible to obtain different decorative effects by using knobby bouclé wool, ribbon, or — in the case of the gingham flowers, for example — bias strips of the same fabric.

Crêpe paper binding: Photograph B shows you how to cut the $\frac{1}{4}$-inch binding strips from a roll of crêpe paper. You will

Right way

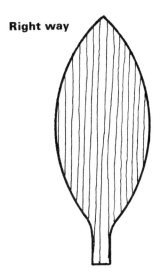

Wrong way

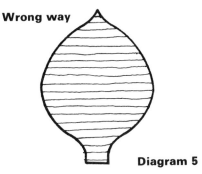

Diagram 5

A

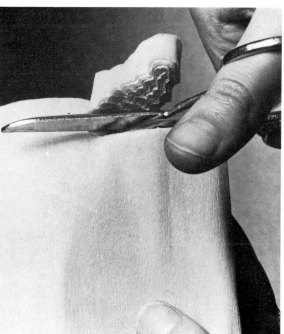

B

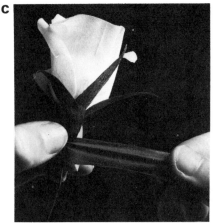

C

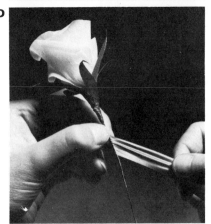

D

need to use very sharp scissors for this in order to cut through a number of thicknesses at once. Hold the roll very tightly in your other hand to prevent it from slipping. Use the same colour of crêpe paper as you have used for the flower calyx or leaves, and always the least obtrusive you can obtain. You will find that we suggest dark green or brown, depending on the colour of the flowers.

Instead of crêpe paper, you can use the floral tape which is obtainable in rolls from florists' shops. This (known as Guttacoll) has a shiny, wax-like finish and is therefore particularly suitable for binding the stems of waxed flowers. It is obtainable in brown, green and white, which we have used, and three other colours. The tape is self-adhesive, so that when you overlap each twist very slightly with the one before, the two edges are sealed where they meet.

Start binding a flower at the top. If using crêpe, put a very small dab of glue on the wrong side of the paper strip, and press the paper on to the calyx. The floral tape does not need adhesive.

Wind the crêpe or tape three times round the flower calyx horizontally, working as tightly as you can. (You will be able to exert slightly more pressure on the tape than on the crêpe paper, which is likely to tear if too roughly treated.) Then work diagonally down the stem, twisting the flower in one hand and holding the strip taut in the other. The action to aim for is that of twisting the flower into the binding strip. Photographs C and D show this clearly. If using crêpe paper, finish off with a tiny dab of glue at the base.

The only exception to this method, when you bind from the base of the stem and work upwards, is in the case of waxed ivy leaves.

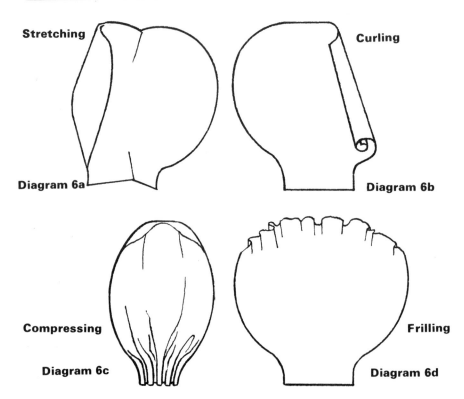

Stretching

Diagram 6a

Curling

Diagram 6b

Compressing

Diagram 6c

Frilling

Diagram 6d